An Altitude SuperGuide

Native Sites
in Western Canada

An Altitude SuperGuide

NATIVE SITES
in Western Canada

●

by Pat Kramer

●

Altitude Publishing Canada Ltd.
The Canadian Rockies
Banff/Canmore, Alberta Canada

PUBLICATION INFORMATION

Altitude Publishing Canada Ltd.
The Canadian Rockies
1408 Railway Avenue, PO Box 1410
Canmore, Alberta T0L 0M0

Canadian Cataloguing in Publication Data
Kramer, Pat
Native Sites in Western Canada

(SuperGuide)
ISBN 1-55153-006-6

1. Indians of North America – Canada, Western – Antiquities – Guidebooks. 2. Canada, Western – Antiquities – Guidebooks. I. Title. II Series.
E78.C2K72 1994   971.2'01
C94-910208-3

Made in Western Canada
Printed and bound in Western Canada by Friesen Printers, Altona, Manitoba.

Altitude GreenTree Program

Altitude Publishing will plant in Western Canada twice as many trees as were used in the manufacturing of this product.

Photographs
Front Cover: Top section of a teepee
  Inset: Totem pole (detail)
Frontispiece: **Headdress from the back**
Back cover: **Competitors relax during a dance competition**

Project Development

Concept/art direction	Stephen Hutchings
Design	Stephen Hutchings
Editing	Maggie Paquet
Maps	Catherine Burgess
Electronic page layout	Stephen Hutchings
	Mary Squario
	Catherine Burgess
Text entry	Michelle Fulton
Electronic file coördination	Sebastian Hutchings
Proofreading	Noeline Bridge
Index	Noeline Bridge
Graphic border artwork	Michelle Kramer
Colour separations	Friesen Printers
Halftones	Stephen Hutchings
Graphics	Stephen Hutchings
Technical assistance	Mark Higenbottam
	Craig Bowman
Financial management	Laurie Smith
Marketing coördinator	Terry Findley

A Note from the Publisher
The world described in Altitude SuperGuides is a unique and fascinating place. It is a world filled with surprise and discovery, beauty and enjoyment, questions and answers. It is a world of people, cities, landscape, animals and wilderness as seen through the eyes of those who live in, work with, and care for this world. The process of describing this world is also a means of defining ourselves.

It is also a world of relationship, where people derive their meaning from a deep and abiding contact with the land – as well as from each other. And it is this sense of relationship that guides all of us at Altitude to ensure that these places continue to survive and evolve in the decades ahead.

Altitude SuperGuides are books intended to be used, as much as read. Like the world they describe, *Altitude SuperGuides* are evolving, adapting and growing. Please write to us with your comments and observations, and we will do our best to incorporate your ideas into future editions of these books.

Stephen Hutchings,
Publisher.

CONTENTS

ABOUT THIS BOOK

There are many sites in western Canada where visitors are invited to glimpse native people and their heritage. Several of these attractions are owned and operated by native communities. A few are owned by native entrepreneurs; others are partnerships between native and non-native people. Many are protected under park or heritage legislation; others are under a museum's jurisdiction. Non-native tour operators and museum curators are increasingly interested in consulting with native people to review the accuracy of their presentations. Many non-native groups and associations express a desire to preserve native culture and are supportive of accuracy in portraying the First Nations' version of history.

This book supports the sincere efforts of all these people. However, its prime intent is to heed the voices of First Nations people themselves. Native people do not belong to the past; they are part of the present and the future. Of course, their history has left vibrant traces on the landscape, but it is their present that illuminates our lives.

This book supports and lists native-owned operations first and top quality non-native operations

Native culture in western Canada is alive and well. During pow-wows and other celebrations, past traditions are revitalized and integrated into the realities of the present.

next. There are excellent sites in both domains. Readers are encouraged to buy authentic native-made arts and crafts, to support native-run operations, to visit heritage attractions, and to encourage all people—native and non-native—to work hard to bring visitors an accurate, entertaining experience.

*Walk in our moccasins
the trail from our past,
Live with us in the here
and now,
Talk with us by the fire
of the days to come.*

—Greetings from the
Aboriginal Nations of
Canada, Expo '67

All sites listed here are open to the public. Sites that glorify skirmishes between natives and settlers are omitted; a few spiritual sites are mentioned—but not located; fur-trading posts and forts are mentioned briefly.

The purpose of most entries is to discuss native-themed sites of interest to travellers; the purpose of other sections is to recap why they are of interest. Along with a few quick sections to refresh the memory, each entry reveals exactly how to acquire access to specific sites—complete with addresses and telephone numbers.

For the record, the follow-

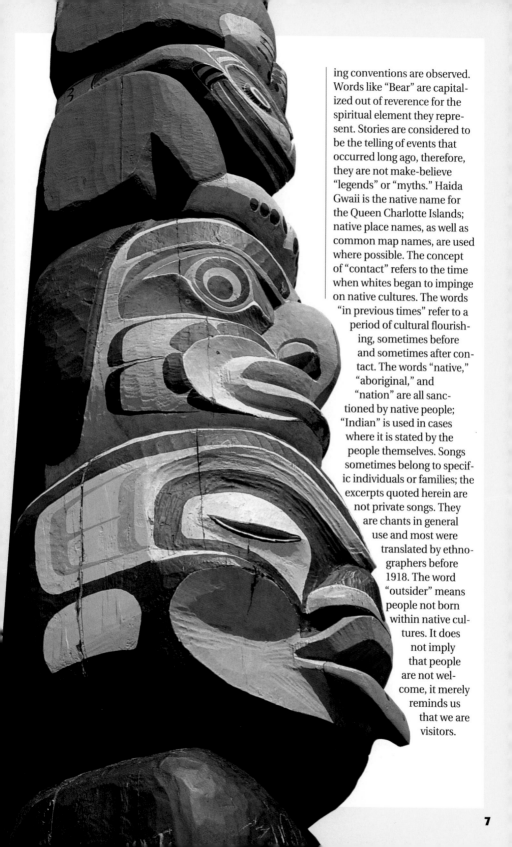

ing conventions are observed. Words like "Bear" are capitalized out of reverence for the spiritual element they represent. Stories are considered to be the telling of events that occurred long ago, therefore, they are not make-believe "legends" or "myths." Haida Gwaii is the native name for the Queen Charlotte Islands; native place names, as well as common map names, are used where possible. The concept of "contact" refers to the time when whites began to impinge on native cultures. The words "in previous times" refer to a period of cultural flourishing, sometimes before and sometimes after contact. The words "native," "aboriginal," and "nation" are all sanctioned by native people; "Indian" is used in cases where it is stated by the people themselves. Songs sometimes belong to specific individuals or families; the excerpts quoted herein are not private songs. They are chants in general use and most were translated by ethnographers before 1918. The word "outsider" means people not born within native cultures. It does not imply that people are not welcome, it merely reminds us that we are visitors.

FIRST NATIONS PARTICIPATION IN CREATING THIS BOOK

The First Nations Tourism Association is dedicated to the promotion and development of First Nations tourism products and services ... while ensuring cultural integrity is honoured and respected.

Sincere thanks are due to the many native people across British Columbia and Alberta who participated in compiling this book—especially the First Nations Tourism Association. Particular gratitude is directed towards those who took the time to give directions, grant interviews, retell stories, share traditions, and make suggestions. Each native tourism operator provided the author with information, then reviewed their listing. Members from the Board of Directors of the First Nations Tourism Association kindly reviewed the recounting of native history and general cultural statements. These collaborations resulted in several suggestions. All were gratefully received, carefully considered, and incorporated into the text.

Recognition is also due to Stephen Hutchings of Altitude Publishing and his staff, all of whom are dedicated to the production of books that reflect an extra measure of sensitivity to the environment and people of western Canada. This book is enthusiastically dedicated to all readers who want to know Father Sky, Mother Earth, and the fascinating people in between.

For membership in or information about the First Nations Tourism Association and its activities, please telephone (604) 769-4499 or fax (604) 769-4866.

When someone finds a feather, it is time to take up wings and travel to strange lands. Why else would the bird have donated it? So too, each feather of information in this book is yours—to take on your own journey.

Access to Museums and Protected Heritage Sites

The most notable cultural centres inwestern Canada operated by native people include the U'mista Cultural Centre in Alert Bay, the Duncan Heritage Centre on Vancouver Island, 'Ksan Indian Village near New Hazelton, and the Head-Smashed-In Interpretive Centre near Fort McLeod. The author has chosen to emphasize western Canadian native-run museums or heritage centres first, and top quality non-native museums second.

Definitive and well-researched collections of western Canadian native artifacts are found at the Royal British Columbia Museum in Victoria, the Museum of Anthropology at UBC in Vancouver, the Glenbow Museum in Calgary, and the Provincial Museum in Edmonton. There are several listings for small artifact collections at regional museums.

Most of the heritage sites listed in this book are protected by various authorities. The UNESCO World Heritage Site program protects *in situ* for educational purposes the Head-Smashed-In buffalo jump in southern Alberta and Ninstints abandoned village in Haida Gwaii. The Cana-

The Glenbow Museum in Calgary displays native regalia, clothing and headdresses. Buckskin items are kept white with regular chalk dustings.

The Museum of Anthropology at the University of British Columbia in Vancouver houses a definitive collection of west coast totem poles and coastal peoples' artifacts. The Giant Woodpecker figure prominent here was once part of a house entrance.

dian Federal Heritage Program protects the Kitwanga Totem Pole Sites, Battle Hill, and 'Ksan village in British Columbia. Parks Canada is responsible for Elk Island National Park and Wood Buffalo National Park, both of which are reserves for buffalo herds. The Salmonid

Enhancement Program, a joint federal-provincial program, protects certain salmon runs in British Columbia.

Research Facilities: Alberta and B. C.

Alberta Archives	Edmonton
British Columbia Archives	Victoria
First Nations House of Learning, UBC	Vancouver
Glenbow Archives and Museum	Calgary
Museum of Anthropology	Vancouver
Native Studies Research, Simon Fraser Univ	Vancouver
Okanagan Indian Education Project	Penticton
Secwepemc Cultural Society	Kamloops
U'mista Cultural Centre	Alert Bay
University of Alberta, Native Studies	Edmonton

Information is available through the
First Nations Tourism Association, (604) 769-4499

ACCESS TO AUTHENTIC NATIVE ARTS

Several galleries and craft stores in western Canada are now under native ownership. Many well-known older establishments, though not native–owned, have had ongoing dealings with native artists for many years. In both cases, the reader is asked to purchase authentic native-made goods through these sources. Native artists benefit from the sale of their goods through all of these outlets.

In general terms, western Canada has a good record for merchandising arts and craft items that are actually created by native people. These are available through art galleries, museum gift shops, and dedicated native craft distribution outlets. Unfortunately, department stores and "tourist souvenir" shops are the least likely places to find genuine items. At present, there is no accepted authentication mark or label for genuine native-made items, except in the case of Cowichan sweaters. These display the trademark "Cowichan Indian Knit."

The outlets listed in this book have a reputation for distributing genuine native-made handicrafts and good quality works of art. Readers who take the time to search out these outlets are generally assured of first rate items that are hand made by native artisans.

For those unfamiliar with natives arts in western Canada, the most desirable BC items are said to be Cowichan sweaters, engraved silver jewellry, limited edition prints, wooden masks, and serving

Calvin Hunt, a carver from the illustrious Hunt clan, reaches deep into the mystic stories told in his culture to empower his masks with movement and life.

dishes. In Alberta, excellence is found in baskets, buckskin mocassins, outdoor clothing, and beadwork items. There is a new movement in prairie-art prints. In the north, Inuit soapstone sculpture and prints are legendary. Pottery is the forté of native groups elsewhere.

My teachers? Who could teach me this? Only legends.
—Norval Morriseau, native artist, 1960

ACCESS TO NATIVE GATHERINGS

I t is through attending public gatherings that many visitors experience their closest encounters with First Nations people and culture. Museums contain collections of things; parks and reserves show the land as it was before contact. Only native gatherings present the people themselves.

In the course of a year, native people put on many functions. Depending upon their traditions, there are memorial services, naming ceremonies, weddings, and meetings. There are potlatches, dinners, and dances. Most of these ceremonies are private.

Festivities that are open to the public are listed in this book. Gatherings of the Nations, Totem Pole Raisings, and Powwows are impressive spectacles and the public is graciously invited. Sometimes a fee is charged. The elders may hold private ceremonies before the celebrations, but there is ample opportunity for the public to listen to the drumbeat of the nations during the public part of these celebrations. The trick to being part of these activities is to make advance inquiries.

In British Columbia, the Kwagiulth Dancers listen while the moderator explains upcoming dances to the audience.

Powwow dancer in Alberta

Native Gatherings

To obtain a list of native gatherings in Western Canada:

For British Columbia, contact Visitor Services, BC Tourism Division, 1117 Wharf St, Victoria, BC V8W 2Z2, (604) 387-6371, 1-800-663-6000, fax (604) 356-8246.

For Alberta, contact Alberta Tourism, 10155 102 St., Edmonton, AB T5J 4L6, (403) 427-4321, 1-800-661-8888, fax (403) 427-0867.

In Alberta, at the Peigan Powwow, a group of prairie dancers listens to their elders' opening prayers and speeches before the dancing competition begins.

This map shows the Native Sites SuperGuide areas in relation to the provinces of British Columbia and Alberta. The four areas are colour-keyed accordingly throughout the book.

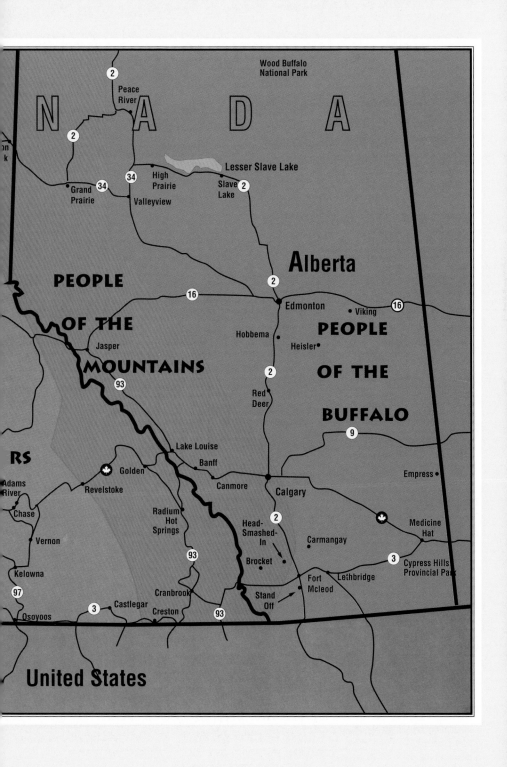

PEOPLE OF THE SALMON

Many parts of British Columbia have not changed from the time when Eagle was a brother and humans acted in harmony together. The setting sun illuminates the ocean and forest setting—home to the aboriginal peoples of the northwest Pacific coast.

Anthropologists speculate that stable communities have existed along the northwest Pacific coast for about 10,000 years—roughly since the civilization of the Egyptians. Over that period, a three-tiered social system evolved: nobles, commoners, and slaves. Nobles lived a luxurious life and enjoyed wealth, not for the sake of accumulation, but for the prestige of giving it away. Commoners were hunters, gatherers, and artisans, who traded goods. By contrast, slaves lived a miserable existence. They were seized along with booty during periodic wars.

Today, native people are acutely aware of their ancestry. They continue to respect the struggle of captives in their family lineages. Native communities rejoice when the descendant of a captive returns to visit their ancestral home.

Northwest Pacific coast natives were primarily fishers, hunters, and gatherers. However, they developed a social structure much like an agricultural society. Some experts say their social structure resulted from an assured food supply, especially the annual run, of salmon. Similiar to an agricultural harvest, thousands of salmon were caught and dried each year. Additionally, the ocean yielded shellfish and the occasional whale carcass.

Land hunters stalked elk, deer, moose, and bear. Others gathered wild berries, roots, and tubers.

From this plenty, thriving societies evolved. Artisans had time to build bighouses, make ocean-going canoes, and prepare for elaborate festivals. The natural abundance of the region made possible a sharing tradition that was embodied formally in the Potlatch.

People of the Salmon

FAMILIAR NAME	ALTERNATE NEW NAMES
Bella Bella	Heiltsuk
Bella Coola	Nuxälk
Kwakiutl, Kwagiulth	Kwakwaka'wakw'
Nootka	Nuu-chah-nulth
Tlingit, Tlinkits, Chilkat	Tlingit
Tsimshian, Niska	Nisga'a, Gitksan

In this book, the new name is used wherever possible. But where there might be confusion, such as in a historic description, the familiar name is used.

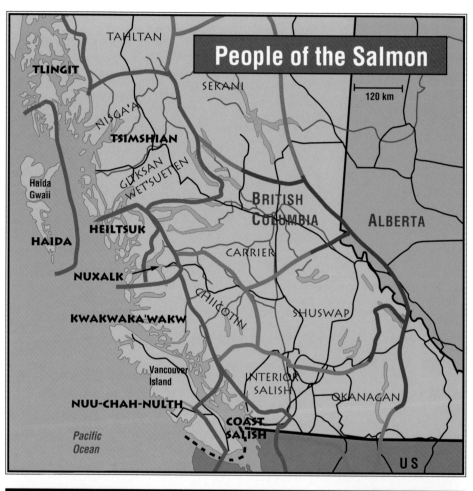

People of the Salmon

TAHLTAN

TLINGIT

SEKANI

120 km

NISGA'A

TSIMSHIAN

Haida
Gwaii

GITKSAN
WET'SUET'EN

BRITISH
COLUMBIA

ALBERTA

HEILTSUK

CARRIER

HAIDA

NUXALK

CHILCOTIN

SHUSWAP

KWAKWAKA'WAKW

Vancouver
Island

INTERIOR
SALISH

OKANAGAN

NUU-CHAH-NULTH

COAST
SALISH

Pacific
Ocean

US

First Nations Tourism Consultant

In 1993, the British Columbia Ministry of Tourism began to assess the rapid growth of native-owned tourism operations within the province. **Mr. Gary Johnston**, a Coast Salish and a Director of the First Nations Tourism Association, was contracted to spearhead an inventory. Johnston found the results quite gratifying. "There are now 182 native-owned businesses directly involved in B.C.'s tourism industry. These include a regional airline, a fishing lodge, two heritage centres, five resorts, and 30 campgrounds. However, not every native-owned business carries on business with a native theme. Some visitors never suspect that the guest services they receive are provided through a tribal council or by a group of native entrepreneurs," Johnston says.

Dwelling Type: The Longhouse

Native people refer to these structures either as "longhouses" or "bighouses." Planks were split off cedar trees using wood (usually yew or ironwood) and antler wedges. These simulated plankhouses are found outside the Museum of Anthropology at UBC in Vancouver.

The coastal aboriginals of British Columbia did not live in teepees. Drawing on an abundant supply of cedar trees, they built rectangular houses of post-and-beam construction, today referred to as bighouses or longhouses. Houses in the north were about 275 square metres (3,000 square feet) in area; houses in the south much larger—up to about 2800 square metres (30,000 square feet). Front and back framing poles held up a central ridgepole; the walls and slightly pitched roof were made of flat cedar planks. Oval doorways were small to prevent drafts. Some designs called for a raised floor around the inside perimeter. Firepits were built directly on the ground. Square openings in the roof permitted smoke to clear and a moveable cover diverted rain from the smoke hole. Loose stones placed on the roof kept the shingles from flying off.

Each family was responsible for a number of planks. When a community moved, the beams were left standing and the planks (walls) were transported to the new location.

Each bighouse could easily accommodate 50 to 200 people, usually members of a single clan related through the female line, or the male and female lines. Most families informally separated their living areas with piled-up wooden chests. These were used to store belongings. Walls were hung with hunting implements and baby cradles. Privacy was at a minimum except for certain elders, who merited walled-off sleeping quarters. Important Haida bighouses had names, such as "clouds bump up against it as they pass over", or "house people are ashamed to look at as it is so overpoweringly great."

A single village consisted of about 50 of these buildings. A series of villages might house up to 30,000 loosely related individuals. The owner of the house supervised the activities of the house members.

Families usually spent the coldest part of the year in their plankhouse community and

> *I am the only chief. My house always thunders.*
> — Chant, Nuu-chah-nulth

Traditional longhouses have served as the inspiration for modern band community facilities.

moved nearer the ocean in summer. The Interior Salish built in-ground pithouses for extra cold winters.

Winter Dances were deeply spiritual and an important part of the annual cycle of events. Massive potlatches took place when events, such as important deaths or births, warranted. During summer, some people set up temporary camps or alternate plankhouse communities where the fishing was good; some set up shelters near berry patches; some camped out on the beach beside productive clam and oyster beds. Each production area was controlled by a specific family. They traded their goods with others. However, all able-bodied adults assembled to help with the salmon harvest. When winter winds again blew in from the ocean, everyone returned to the villages.

A totem pole at the front door acted as the family's coat of arms. Strangers could decipher a totem pole and thus avoid houses that belonged to unfriendly clans. If the pole displayed familiar markings, strangers were welcome to board there for extended periods.

After contact, non-native strangers sometimes entered houses that were inappropriate to them. A few elders resorted to painting English signs on their bighouses. In 1901, one large Kwagiulth bighouse displayed a neatly lettered sign: "He is one of the head chiefs of all tribes in this country. White man can get information" —(that is, obtain information before presuming to enter).

A Camera Safari: Modern Plankhouses

Visitors may view the exteriors of modern plankhouses in use today. Some are referred to as bighouses, others as longhouses.

For information on British Columbia bighouse interiors open to the public, ask for the Tourism Product Guide, Native Cultural Products and Events No. 31, BC Ministry of Tourism, (604) 660-2861, fax (604) 660-

Traditional Bighouses, outdoors	6393 NW Marine Dr, Vancouver
Native Education Centre	283 E 5th Ave, Vancouver
Traditional and Modern Bighouses	Welch St, North Vancouver
Coqualeetza Cultural Centre	Sardis
Thunderbird Bighouse	Thunderbird Park, Victoria
Bighouse, simulation	Royal BC Museum, Victoria
Four Longhouses	Native Heritage Centre, Duncan
Lau,Welnew Tribal School	Brentwood Bay
Kwagiulth Museum	Quadra Island
U'mista Cultural Centre	Alert Bay
Traditional and Modern Bighouses	Bella Coola
Eight Bighouses	'Ksan Village, New Hazelton
Abandoned Bighouse Village	Ninstints, Haida Gwaii

Salmon: the Vital Harvest

ABOVE: Fresh salmon are spread out with alderwood slats at the Tsa•Kwa•Luten Lodge on Quadra Island. INSET: Ancient pictographs are occasionally found near productive salmon runs. Their exact meaning is lost in time but vibrant colours hint at old spirit brothers and sisters who wished to share wisdom with others.

Aboriginal rock paintings attest to the longstanding importance of salmon, both to the Pacific coastal region and along the rivers of the interior. By providing native people with a seemingly inexhaustible and recurring food source, the salmon's cyclical return remains the underpinning of aboriginal life.

The anadromous lifecycle of Pacific salmon is remarkable. Most species spend their adult life in saltwater and return to breed in freshwater. One exception is a landlocked variety, the kokanee. It spends all its life in freshwater.

Ocean dwelling chum, chinook, coho, sockeye, and springs spawn only once, then die a few days later. Upon entering fresh water, several species develop hooked snouts, humpbacks, and skin lesions; sockeye turn a bright red colour. Females excavate a nest, males immediately release milt alongside. The females flip gravel from the stream bed to cover their eggs. Depending upon the species and the temperature of the surrounding waters, the tiny fry, called alevins, emerge from one to five months later.

Today, private and government-run hatchery facilities

Traditional Native Fishing Areas in Seasonal Use Today

Native salmon camps are usually in use from mid-July through August. Outsiders may visit if they stay well back from anglers at work. Information is available from BC Travel Info-Centres: Farwell or Lillooet (604) 392-2226, 1-800-663-5885; or Moricetown (604) 847-5227.

Farwell Canyon near Williams Lake	Spearing, drying nearby
The Old Bridge at Lillooet	Netting, drying
Moricetown near Terrace	Spearing, drying nearby

may visit spawning rivers and enhancement channels to witness salmon searching out their mates in shallow, running waters. See box on page 61 for enhancement channel and major spawning river listings.

Salmon grow large in the mighty ocean. Their silvery sides flash in shallow freshwater streams as they return for procreation.

employ staff to capture a portion of the returning adults, remove their eggs and milt, then incubate the fertilized eggs in trays. In comparison with the wild, this early intervention increases survival rates about ten-fold. However, there are concerns. Over their entire lifespan, hatchery-bred fry may display a weaker constitution. While all human/wildlife interventions are subject to error, the hatchery program is a calculated attempt to compensate for impingement on salmon stocks. Most importantly of all, the continued preservation of natural spawning habitats remains a critical issue.

As an adjunct to traditional aboriginal ways and the inculcation of deep respect for all life, native bands operate several B.C. hatcheries in remote areas of the province. Coastal and interior native groups also continue to be experts at harvesting salmon. In previous times, many bands erected fish weirs—underwater branch-link fences. Others perfected braided dipnets made of nettle fibres attached to frames. Still others used spears, wicker, funnel traps, or hooks made of bone or hardwood. Today, natives retain traditional rights to gaff salmon or to set permanent nets onshore. Tons of salmon are fileted, hung to dry on racks, or smoked inside improvised shelters.

In season, outsiders can observe native salmon-drying camps in certain areas, or they

In a native smokehouse, whole salmon are prepared using time honoured methods. In order to render just the right taste and the correct degree of dryness, firewood is cut from specific species of alder trees

Public Viewing of Fish Enhancement Programs

All hatcheries, native and non-native, are open to the public year round. Spawning channels are open in season—usually a two-week period between late July and December. When viewing fish in the wilderness, stay near roadways. Bears are active around wilderness spawning areas. People, pets, and debris must remain out of the water; fish are unable to spawn in the presence of unusual scents. An information booklet detailing the location of salmon hatcheries and channels is available, *Where and When to See Salmon*, from Fisheries and Oceans Publications, Suite 400, 555 West Hastings, Vancouver, BC V6B 5G3, (604) 666-0384. To participate in the visitor program at six provincial sports fish hatcheries contact any of thethe Fish Culture Section, 780 Blanshard Street, Victoria, BC V8V 1X4, (604) 387-9698.

CEDAR: SOFT WOOD OF MANY USES

The cedar is an extraordinarily useful tree. Its bark separates easily into strips, yet the wood holds a firm edge when carved. Feathery cedar leaves have a pleasant fragrance.

Western Red Cedar and Yellow Cedar have played a central role in the lifestyles of coastal people for thousands of years. Each part of these trees was used for a wide variety of products.

Strips of cedar pulled from an inner bark layer were woven into floor mats, funnel-shaped fish traps, or baskets for berrypickers. With a skeleton of branches, woven mats could be transformed into a smokehouse or a temporary summer shelter.

Cedar twigs from the cedar were dried, hammered, and rolled into ropes. Narrow strands were woven into fish-nets; thicker plaits were used to construct suspension bridges.

Several kinds of clothing were fashioned from both red and yellow cedar strips. Although women wore cedar skirts year-round, men preferred to go naked in summer. In the rainy season, all welcomed rain capes, overgarments with belts, and wide-brimmed rain hats. Clothing made from cedar was bulky. It was supplemented with animal skin garments and robes spun from dog hair or mountain goat fleece.

*For there is nothing for which
you cannot be used.
For you are willing to give
us your dress,
I pray you, friend, not to
feel angry,
For what I am going to do to you.*
—Prayer to a Young Cedar, Kwakwaka'wakw'

Dishes, pots, and some utensils were made of cedar wood. Wooden dishes carved into the shapes of eagles or

bears were used for serving. Yellow cedar was particularily prized for this purpose. In some cases, hollowed logs became giant serving dishes. They were filled with food to feed a crowd of hundreds at a potlatch. Neutral-tasting alderwood was the preferred wood for making spoons. Mountain goat horns were fashioned into large serving ladles.

The watertight bent cedar box was a special type of cooking pot. A flat cedar piece was scored, then folded, and fastened with pegs on one edge. Each box held about 15 litres of water. Using a pair of tongs, red-hot rocks were put in to boil the water. Then food was added to cook. In some cases, larger bent boxes were painted, a lid was fashioned, and they were used to store a family's ceremonial goods.

Skilled carpenters made use of bone or elk horn chisels and D-shaped adze tools to manufacture large war canoes.

Whole cedar logs were felled by a burn-through method.

Hot rocks were added to cook out the heartwood, and sticks were wedged between the sides to widen the interior. The Nuu-chah-nulth were especially adept at this practice. Forty to fifty paddlers propelled these vessels on long whale-hunting expeditions.

Yellow cedar is still preferred for totem poles and masks. The wood carves like butter and holds a firm edge when completed.

Finally, massive bighouses were made of red cedar log frames and plank walls. If a building was abandoned, the walls and roof were removed, leaving the post-and-beam frame standing alone. When the clan returned, the walls and roof panels were quickly reconstructed.

Today, hikers can find live cedar trees showing a distinctive rectangular scar, usually on one side of the lower trunk. Cedar strips were removed from these areas in a very careful way so the tree could still live and grow. These culturally modified cedars are protected in legislation and cannot be cut down. They stand to remind us of the care taken to preserve nature, even while using its products.

Chehltn, A Cedar Carver

"When I am chewed up by the rat race, I make my knife chew up the cedar, and I relax," says **Brian Williams**. Called *Chehltn* in his own tongue, Williams believes in the meaning of his native name: "seeking it."

Coast Salish by birth and a member of the Squamish Band, Chehltn produces carved talking sticks and traditional wooden ornaments. Talking sticks are

about the size of a walking cane. Much like a judge's gavel, they signify that a person has the right to speak. At a large gathering, those who hold the stick, command the floor.

William's work is available from Khot-La-Cha Handicrafts, 270 Whonoak Street, North Vancouver, BC, (604) 987-3339.

TOTEM POLES: FAMILY COATS OF ARMS

The figure of the eagle tells of a creature soaring aloft on outstretched wings, climbing higher than the human eye can see, soaring in unchallenged freedom over the vast domain of earth and sky.

Totem pole carving is an art form highly developed by northwest Pacific coast natives.

Totems usually feature a series of two to five vertically placed symbolic figures. These figures primarily depict a clan's names, its coat of arms, and family history. Totems were never worshipped.

To the present, old family clans die out and new ones are created. For example, in the 1800s, the Double Eagle Imperial Coat of Arms was carried by Russian traders and the Beaver emblem was used by the Hudson's Bay Company. Each of these fur trader symbols evolved into a clan surname. Natives of the time who traded with these outsiders signified their occupation by adopting "Double

Eagle" or "Beaver" as part of their names. These names were then rendered into figures and depicted on their totem poles.

Totems are carved to serve a purpose. A memorial pole remembers a great person through his or her names and symbolic figures; a mortuary pole holds the remains of a former elder or chief; a

commemorative pole recalls a great happening. The tallest totem used to stand in front of the house of the most powerful chief. Lesser chiefs were sometimes forced to shorten their poles. Even inside the plankhouse, the structural posts were carved to illustrate popular narratives. On long winter nights, by the light of the fire, these decorated house

To Commission a Full Size Totem Pole

Copper Maker Studio
Hunt Family, Box 755,
Port Hardy, BC V0N 2Z0,
(604) 949-8491
Hy'emass House
Bill Helin, 468 Island Highway,
Box 883, Parksville, BC V9P 2G6,
(604) 248-2423,
fax (604) 248-4844
Krentz Forest Products
Richard Krentz, Box 733,

Campbell River, BC V9W 6J3,
(604) 286-0120,
fax (604) 286-3639
Native Heritage Centre
200 Cowichan Way, Duncan, BC
V9L 4T8, (604) 746-8119,
fax (604) 746-4143
Cherry Point Studio
William Kuhnley, Nitinat,
Vancouver Island, BC
(604) 736-4526

posts served as scenic backdrops for dances and stories. The door opening of a house might also be carved with figures all around, or it might be framed with a carved house portal.

Occasionally, totem figures teach lessons or recall events. For example, on one pole, the ﹍ncept of "harmony" is suggested by a set of interlocking humans. On another pole, a crying woman holding a grouse recalls an unusual famine. A few totem figures were used to shame others. For example, if a person was depicted upside down or with backwards feet, the intention was to embarrass the person into repaying a debt.

Supernatural animals are carved onto a great number of poles. Giant Woodpecker is common in the north and

Thunderbird is popular in the south. Long ago in the mists of time, Bear, Wolf, and Beaver transformed into humans and all founded human families. These animal figures continue to signify ancient family names. Raven, a mischievous bird-human, is a popular humourous or trickster figure. Raven discovered the first-ever humans crammed inside a clam shell. Another time, Raven annoyed the human race by stealing the sun and the moon.

A large totem pole once stood outside each plank house. Strangers entering a village studied each pole, primarily to identify the family members who lived inside.

Most tribes were matrilineal, so women's as well as men's crests appeared. By identifying the figures related to their own clan totems, strangers could determine if it was proper for them to enter a house.

Today, new poles are carved with all the solemnity of their predecessors. Old poles are duplicated under traditional rules. The names of modern carvers are honoured: Norman Tait, the Hunt family, Richard Krentz, Mungo Martin. Carvers of old are remembered by the clan-figures they carved into their totems, but their personal names are lost in time.

Mark George: Totem Carver

Mark George learned to whit-tle at the side of his brothers and their friends. At first he produced wooden bowls and talking sticks. Later, his works became noted for abalone shell inlays.

Coast Salish Mark George is now beginning to carve full-sized poles. Before deciding on a design, he researches the interests of the people who will own the pole. "White people prefer easy-to-interpret animals," he says, "but I carve my own Wolf crest only on poles that I make for my own people." Depending upon its size and complexity, a pole takes from two to eight months to construct.

George chips away at a log of yellow cedar, transforming it, liberating the forms trapped in the log. "I feel best when the children watch me because they

are not afraid to ask questions. I even get them to paint the pole." Anxious to pass on his skills to the next generation, George's totems are special. They show the hands of the youngsters he allows to help with the painting. George's work is available through Mark George Carvings, (604) 924-1066.

THE COWICHAN SWEATER: A NATIVE KNIT ORIGINAL

Genuine Cowichan sweaters in natural shades of white, grey, black, and brown have been constructed from hand-spun wools in the same manner for a century. Adapted from Icelandic or Scottish knitting, west coast natives today use original designs: the Eagle, Twin Eagle, Deer, Whale, or the popular Thunderbird.

Although native people have long excelled in weaving blankets from mountain goat wool knowledge of knitting-in-the-round may have arrived via the nuns from the log convent of St. Ann's, the Scottish pioneer Jeremina Colvin from Hill Bank, or from Japanese women on visiting gillnetters. Whatever the origin, native women now have a century of skill in spinning lanolin-rich wools and knitting these distinctive bulky garments.

Today,

the water-resistant sweaters, toques, mitts, and scarves are cherished by outdoors people. A favoured Cowichan sweater is worn, patched, and used until it collapses from decades of overuse. The warm woolies have grown in stature to the point where visiting government dignitaries, celebrities, and royals collect them as a prized Canadian gift.

Cowichan means land warmed by the sun.
—Khowutzun

Imitation sweaters, sometimes erroneously rendered in pastel blues, now flood the Japanese market. None approaches the quality of the natural-coloured originals, each hand-made by a *Khowutzun* native knitter from Vancouver Island or the Lower Mainland. Together, they turn out about 800 authentic wool sweaters each month.

Look for the label with a registration number indicating a genuine "Cowichan Indian Knit." Cowichan sweaters may be obtained from several sources, including Sasquatch Trading Mail Order Department, 1233 Government Street, Victoria, BC V8W 1Y6, (604) 386-9033; or Authentic Cowichan Knits, 424 West 3rd Street, North Vancouver, BC V7M 1G7, (604) 988-4735.

When I start to fly, the thunder resounds throughout the world.
—War Song, Kwakwaka'wakw'

In a time long ago, it is said that animals shared many of the same qualities as people. Once a giant Killer Whale ate all the salmon in the ocean. Humans began to starve. Although the chiefs begged the Whale to leave, it repeatedly mocked them. Finally, a congress of the greatest chiefs was convened. After a time, a great wind blew in from the sea. Lightning flashed. They felt the presence of an invisible spirit. "If I were to help you, what will you do for me?" it asked. The chiefs promised, for all time, to reproduce the spirit's likeness as a sign of admiration.

Thus, satisfied with their promises, Thunderbird appeared. He was an enormous manifestation with lightning flashing from his pointed talons and thunder rolling from his sun-blocking wings.

Snatching up the Killer Whale, the raptor spirit dropped it onto the land where it solidified into a mountain. Native carvers have kept their word since. That is why Thunderbird is seen atop many totem poles.

The Stones are Speaking

An archaeological site contains evidence of past cultures. For more information about archaeology in British Columbia, or about joining an archaeological dig, contact the Archaeology Branch, Legislative Buildings, Victoria, BC V8V 1X4; The Archaeological Society of BC, Box 520, Station A, Vancouver BC V6C 2N3; the Underwater Archaeological Society of BC, c/o Maritime Museum, 1905 Ogden St, Vancouver BC V6J 1A3; or the Heritage Society of BC, 411 Dunsmuir Street, Vancouver BC V6B 1X4.

WHERE NATIVES GATHER: BRITISH COLUMBIA

Wolf dancers echo the rhythmic lines of their animal mentors.

Each year, B.C. native communities put on a series of festivals. Most gatherings take place between mid-May and September. Some last one day; others are longer. The public is invited to join these celebrations, though the events are run solely for the perpetuation of First Nations cultures.

Visitors can expect different activities, depending upon the nature of the event. Cultural festivals and powwows are a combination of plays, songs, salmon barbeques, and dances. Sports days may revolve around fastball tournaments. A rodeo is a cowboy-horse event, and elders' gatherings consist of long speeches. Canoe races feature racing heats. Outdoor folksingers are the main entertainers at concerts. A lahal tournament is a traditional

guessing game. The object is to determine which team is hiding marked bones while singers confuse the guessers.

Noteworthy B.C. gatherings include Powwows at Chilliwack, Chase, the Squamish Nation powwow in Vancouver, the First People's Festival in Victoria, the Kamloopa Powwow at Kamloops, and the all-native Sugarcane Rodeo at Williams Lake.

In a different vein, B.C. museums periodically engage

native people to put on demonstrations. During these sessions, native artists lecture, create works of art, or perform dances.

The secret to witnessing these festivals or demonstrations, is timing. Visitors should plan ahead, travel to the community, find the exact site, and be patient while the participants prepare. The colour and splendour are worth the effort.

B.C. Native Gatherings

For a list of annual B.C. First Nations events or museum demonstrations, contact the First Nations Tourism Association, (604) 769-4499; BC Tourism, 1117 Wharf Street, Victoria, BC V8W 2Z2, (604) 387-6371; or the British Columbia Museums Association, 606 Superior Street, Victoria, V8V 1V1, (604) 387-

3701. To arrange a native dance troupe or traditional foods for a large group, contact Sharing the Spirit, Canpac Marketing, 303, 345 Michigan Street, Victoria BC V8V 1R7, (604) 389-1718, fax (604) 389-0588; or Prime Talent Native Entertainments, (604) 879-6883.

ARTS AND CRAFTS: BRITISH COLUMBIA

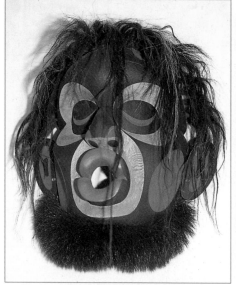

Masks once reserved for use during Winter Dances are now considered an artform in their own right. This mask depicts a frightening character who was said to eat children. Her mouth purses in a kissing motion to attract her victims.

Bill Helin is a Tsimshian from the Lax Kw' Alaams tribe. He hand-engraves gold and silver with tribal crests and characters from ancestral stories, and distributes his works through Hy'emass House in Parksville.

A sense of beauty in everyday living was a fundamental part of northwest Pacific coast life. Although fired pottery was entirely lacking, wooden items served the same purposes. Watertight bent boxes were used for cooking, and cedar serving dishes were intricately carved. Almost all common household articles were carved with ceremonial designs. Creature-figures originally rendered on totems, masks, ocean-going canoes, and wooden food utensils eventually evolved into the distinctive west coast art forms that continue to be valued today.

Traditionally, there are several unique items associat-ed with the Pacific northwest people: massive totem poles, decorated bent boxes, and woven spruce root or cedar hats. In the textile arts, Tlingit (Chilkat) women wove distinctively designed blankets. After contact, button blankets made of red and black wool melton-cloth were embellished with hundreds of shiny abalone shell buttons.

Today, gold and silver jewellry, as well as limited-edition prints are sought after art forms. Masks and wooden carvings continue to be part of the artistic tradition. Native arts are available through art galleries, arts and craft stores, and museum gift shops. Craft shows, where visitors can buy crafts directly from native arti-sans, are held in conjunction with native gatherings such as powwows, pole raisings and cultural festivals.

British Columbia Visitor Information

For information about native experiences and travel information contact: Visitor Services, BC Tourism Division, 1117 Wharf Street, Victoria, BC V8W 2Z2, (604) 387-6371, fax (604) 356-8246; toll-free in North America from Discover British Columbia, 1-800-663-6000. For ferry travel across the Strait of Georgia between the mainland, Vancouver Island, the Gulf Islands, or other small islands, contact BC Ferries, (604) 386-3431, (604) 669-1211.

THUNDERBIRD PARK: VICTORIA

During the early 1950s, totem carving was in danger of becoming a lost art. The totems surrounding the Thunderbird Bighouse were restored or duplicated by Mungo Martin and his team of apprentices. Their work allowed the totem to once again reach out across cultures and time to spread its message.

In 1964, a traditional bighouse was donated in perpetuity to Kwagiulth native Mungo Martin and his family. In a small way, it serves to honour Martin's single-handed contribution to northwest Pacific Coast cultures.

To understand this contribution, it must be recalled that during the early 1900s, the great museums of Europe, Canada, and the United States acquired thousands of ethnographic items. Hundreds of totems were shipped to Berlin, Paris, Washington D.C., and Australia. The lesser poles that were left behind became increasingly dilapidated. In the 1950s, museum staff from the University of British Columbia gradually recognized the declining state of native arts and searched for someone to revitalize old ways.

Mungo Martin from Alert Bay was a master carver who had been taught in secret. He was engaged to duplicate totems based on a declining stock of BC totems. For the rest of his life, he replicated poles, not only from his own culture, but from other tribes as well. By his death in 1965, he had passed on his skills to young carvers, revitalized several traditions, and redis-covered the stories behind many poles.

The outdoor totem display at the Royal BC Museum is always open. The bighouse is open for carving demonstra-tions and during native festivals. Both are located on the corner of Belleville and Douglas streets. Information is available from BC Tourism Visitor Services, 812 Wharf Street, Victoria, BC V8W 1T3, (604) 382-2127, toll free 1-800-663-3883, fax (604) 382-6539. To get to Vancouver Island by ferry contact BC Ferries, (604) 386-3431 or (604) 669-1211.

MUSEUMS: VICTORIA AND AREA

Outside the Royal British Columbia Museum in the heart of Victoria, a series of totem poles, wooden greet-figures, and a dugout canoe are among the large display items that represent the one-time wealth of coastal natives. Inside the museum, numerous artifacts and a full-sized plankhouse, complete with glowing fire, allow visitors to appreciate the comfortable living conditions enjoyed by these people before contact. As much as possible, each native display at the museum is designed to bring alive the feelings behind the items. Drum music plays in the background and scores of wooden masks are dramatically illuminated.

A model of a Tsimshian chief dressed in a woven Chilkat blanket wears a headdress filled with duck down. Chiefs and elders still dance to remind their people of peace, white feathers cascading gracefully around them.

As well as representing coastal groups, the museum features a full scale kekuli pit house, such as those used by interior bands. Fine examples of artifacts and works of art illustrate the tasks which occupied both the coastal and interior native people.

On the museum grounds, the gardens are cultivated with specially chosen botanical specimens. Some of these plants were used as therapies or medicines by native people. A descriptive pamphlet is available on site. The gift shop in the museum is stocked with excellent quality native art and crafts. Next door, the B.C. Archives building stores files that are available for research purposes. Information is available from the Royal British Columbia Museum, 672 Belleville Street, Victoria, BC V8V 1X4; (604) 387-3014, (604) 387-3701.

Additional museums in the area include the Sidney Museum and its collection of native artifacts (604) 656-1322; or the Sooke Regional Museum and its Coast Salish objects, (604) 642-3121.

Spirit of Lekwammen The World's Tallest Totem Pole

Towering 55 metres above Victoria Harbour, the world's tallest totem pole was raised into position on August 17, 1994. The pole is carved from a 300-year-old western red cedar felled by the project coordinator and head carver, Coast Salish Richard Krentz. Native artists from every B.C. coastal nation participated in carving the pole and it was blessed by Chief Norman George and elders of the Songhees Band. Bestowed with the name *Lekwammen*, meaning "land of the winds," the pole was three years from concept to raising. The pole is shown here at the start of the carving process.

The Queen's Baton

The Queen's Baton designed for the 1994 Commonwealth Games is a unique work of native art.

Commissioned by B.C. Hydro, working in partnership with the Native Participation Committee of the XV Commonwealth Games, the Baton represents an artistic and cultural collaboration of aboriginal artists from Vancouver Island First Nations: Charles Elliot, of the Coast Salish Nation; Art Thompson, of the Nuu-Chah-Nulth Nation; and Richard Hunt, of the Kwakwaka'wakw' Nation.

The Queen's Baton carried the message Her Majesty Queen Elizabeth II read during the opening ceremonies, officially starting the Games.

The baton is made in the shape of a traditional soul-catcher, an item that stores an ill person's soul while they recover.

NATIVE ARTS IN VICTORIA

Although her name means "laughing one," Klee Wyck's works are often characterized as brooding or somber.

mily Carr, born in 1871, lived some of her life among native people in remote coastal villages. The Nuu-chah-nulth gave her the name Klee Wyck, which means "the laughing one." She combined her talent, her European training, and the influence of the Nuu-chah-nulth into a unique artistic style. Her family home in Victoria is now restored as a heritage attraction. Emily Carr's works are said to be expressive of a deep spiritual power that evolved from living among aboriginals. Characterized by brooding light and udulating strokes, her works are a repository of intense feeling. The Art Gallery of Greater Victoria, and the Emily Carr Gallery display several of her originals. Most of her works are located at the Vancouver Art Gallery.

To view Emily Carr's works in Victoria, contact Carr House, 207 Government St, (604) 387-4697; Emily Carr Gallery, 1107 Wharf St, (604) 384-3130; or the Art Gallery of Greater Victoria, 1040 Moss St, (604) 384-4104.

Native Arts: Victoria

Alcheringa Fine Art Gallery,
665 Fort Street
(604) 383-8224
Arts of the Raven Gallery,
1015 Douglas Street
(604) 386-3731
Canadian Impressions,
811Government Street
(604) 383-2641
Cowichan Trading Co,
1328 Government Street
(604) 383-0321
Gallery Shop,

1040 Moss Street
(604) 384-7012
Hills Indian Crafts,
1008 Government Street
(604) 385-3911
Indian Craft Shoppe,
905 Government Street
(604) 382-3643
James Bay Trading Co,
1102 Government Street
(604) 388-5477
Northwest Trader,
Suite 65, 560 Johnston Street

(604) 381-6652
Pharos II,
514 Fort Street
(605) 386-5446
Sasquatch Trading Ltd,
1233 Government Street
(604) 386-9033
Sharing the Spirit Gallery,
826 Johnston Street
(604) 380-1436
The Quest,
1023 Government Street
(604) 382-1934

FIRST PEOPLES FESTIVAL: VICTORIA

ABOVE: The pageantry, singing, and activities of large canoe gatherings are not considered re-enactments of the past. Each gathering is a commemorative happening in its own right. INSET: After introductory ceremonies on the water, a long parade of paddlers and coaches winds its way to the Parliament Buildings.

Once each year in August, the Coast Salish, Nuu-chah-nulth, and Kwakwaka'wakw' nations welcome visitors to Victoria in the Salish language, *Matolya*. During this three-day festival, hundreds of aboriginal paddlers, dancers, drummers, and athletes participate in cultural events. The celebration begins with a traditional welcome on the water. A drummer alerts the onlookers that strange canoes have been sighted. While dancers perform on shore, longboats glide into Victoria's Inner Harbour. Smaller scout-canoes paddle out to greet the arriving vessels. When the smaller canoes have encircled the guests, all the boats paddle in together, stopping briefly offshore to raise paddles, sing, and greet the assembled elders. As in earlier days, the scouts determine the true intentions of the arriving flotilla. If the guests are friendly, white feathers are sprinkled onto the water.

Cultural festivities, such as this annual gathering of nations, include a powwow of native drummers and dancers. Up to 400 costumed dancers assemble on the parade grounds. While the dance competitions continue, the Gorge Waterway is the site of the War Canoe races. Native cuisine, such as barbequed salmon, is featured and there is an artist's market. Information is available from the Victoria Native Friendship Centre, 533 Yates Street, Victoria, BC V8W 1K7, (604) 384-3211, fax (604) 384-1586.

Public Native Events: Vancouver Island	
Nimpkish First Nations Sports, Alert Bay,	June
Victor Underwood Water Festival, East Saanich	June
Nuu-chah-nulth Indian Games, Port Alberni	July
Khowutzun Water Sports, Cowichan Bay	July
Annual Elders Gathering, Duncan	August
First Peoples Festival, Victoria	August
Annual Arts Show and Sale, Duncan	November

Special Tours: Departures from Vancouver Island

Adventures West Tours Ltd., 851 Shelbourne Blvd, Campbell River, BC V9W 4Z7, (604) 923-6113, fax (604) 923-6119; by van, a 7-hour tour to the Kwagiulth Museum and Tsa Kwa Luten Lodge.

Alberni Marine Transportation, Box 188, Port Alberni, BC V9Y 7M7, (604) 723-8313, fax (604) 723-8314; by working freighters the *M.V. Lady Rose* or *M.V. Frances Barkley*, 11 hours to Ucluelet, Bamfield, Pacific Rim National Park, and remote villages.

There are several tour operators and two boat transport companies that offer tours into the B.C. wilderness. West Coast Expeditions takes visitors to a remote island to view old totems.

Bluewater Adventures, 202, 1656 Duranleau St, Vancouver, BC V6H 3S4, (604) 684-4575, fax (604) 689-5926; by 68' ketch with staterooms, 7 days exploring remote coastline areas.

Canadian Outback Adventure Company, 206-1110 Hamilton St, Vancouver, BC V6B 2S2, (604) 688-7206, 1-800-565-8732, fax (604) 688-7290; by bikes, rafts, horseback, or 65' ft ketch with staterooms, 18 innovative vacations.

Canadian River Expeditions, #302 3524 West 16th Ave, Vancouver, BC V6R 3C1; (604)738-4449, by inflatable raft or on foot; natural history expedition outfitters; 6- to 12-day tours.

Great Expeditions, 5915 West Boulevard, Vancouver, BC V6M 3X1, (604) 263-1476, 1-800-663-3364; by canoe or wooden cutter, photo-tours of grizzly bears; river or ocean itineraries.

Island Expeditions Co, #368, 916 West Broadway, Vancouver, BC V5Z 1K7, phone and fax, (604) 325-7952, 1-800-667-1630; by kayak, custom trips.

Nootka Sound Service Ltd., Box 57, Gold River, BC V0P 1G0, (604) 283-2325, 1-800-663-1915; by working freighter the *M.V. Uchuck III*, 6 hours to Captain Cook's first landing place and a remote native village; also 2 days to Kyuquot, secluded fishing village.

Robson Bight Charters, Box 99, Sayward, BC V0P 1R0, (604) 282-3833; by 56' motor yacht, 7-hour cruise, whale-watching.

Saanich Native Society, Box 28, Brentwood Bay, BC V0S 1A0, (604) 652-5980; on foot, by arrangement, Lau'Welnew Tribal School traditional bighouse, 1-hour tour.

Sea Orca Expeditions, Box 483, 66 Fir Street, Alert Bay, BC V0N 1A0, (604) 974-5225, (604) 974-2266; by kayak, custom

escorted tours.

Seacoast Expeditions, Box 1412, Victoria, BC V8W 2X2, (604) 383-2254; by Zodiac, whale–watching, 3 hours from Victoria Inner Harbour.

Stubbs Island Charters Ltd., Box 7, Telegraph Cove, BC V0N 3J0, (604) 928-3185, (604) 928-3117; by 60' vessel, orca whale–watching, 6-hour cruise.

Tofino Expeditions, 114, 1857 West 4th Ave, Vancouver, BC V6J 1M4, (604) 737-2030, fax (604) 737-7348; by kayak, 6-day guided expeditions to Clayoquot Sound or Haida Gwaii.

West Coast Expeditions, 1348 Ottawa Ave, West Vancouver, BC V7T 2H5, (604) 926-1110, fax (604) 926-1110; by boat and on land, 6 days group camping, visit with Nuu-chah-nulth people.

Western Wildcat Tours, Box 1162, Nanaimo, BC, V9R 6E7, (604) 753-3234; by backpack or kayak, various tours of Vancouver Island.

Wild Heart Adventures, Site P, C-5, RR4, Nanaimo, BC V9R 5X6, (604) 722-3683, fax (604) 722-2175; by sea kayak, escorted expeditions.

Yuquot Tours, Box 459, Gold River, BC V0P 1G0, (604) 283-7476; on foot, Yuquot National Historic Site, on foot, I hour, visit native people; also with salmon barbecue by special arrangement.

CITY OF TOTEMS: DUNCAN

In 1985, Duncan City Council commissioned two native carvers to create a series of totem poles. One dozen old-growth cedar logs were donated by a logging company. The project began with Cowichan carvers Tom and Douglas LaFortune, joined later by Francis Horne. Under the chisels of the three workers, the poles took shape. As the first year of carving progressed, public interest was ardent and a "City of Totems" program was begun. Each successive year, more totems are added to the collection.

During its third year, Duncan's totem project began to attract international attention. A Maori craftsperson, Tupari Te Whata, arrived to work alongside local carvers. Under the direction of master carver Richard Hunt, and with Te Whata's involvement, the 1987 work team holds a record; they carved the world's thickest totem. Named Te Awhio Whio, "The King of the Cedar Forest," the figure of Cedar Man is said to be transforming out of the log. With an impressive diameter of 2 metres, it stands near Duncan's City Hall.

By 1990, a collection of 32 more painted totems occupied city parks, public squares, and lined the sides of the highway. Duncan's totems tend to average about 4.5 m in height, the size of a bighouse interior framing post.

The Thunderbird over a Whale is a common totem

In previous times, poles this size were used as interior house posts. Although totems were never worshipped, their strength derives not from the wood itself but from the quality that dwells within.

subject. Interpreted in a different way by each group of carvers, the eagle-like figure clutching a whale is a story central to several native groups. But not every winged creature topping a totem pole is Thunderbird; only mystical Thunderbird has curly ears. Eagles have a plain head.

Flamboyant Thunderbird's reputation as the majestic monarch of the skies has spread far and wide. The winged raptor is found topping poles as far away as Alberta and Ontario.

According to a local story, Whale and Wolf are two forms of the same animal spirit. It is

said there is a rock near Duncan where whales come to rub themselves. There they are transformed into wolves so they can hunt on the land.

The word "totem" may be derived from the Chippewa word *ototemen* which signifies "kinfolk." Because animals were believed to embody qualities similar to humans, an animal could therefore become a symbol for a family. Whites originally saw totem figures as symbols of imaginary beings; natives saw them as likenesses of their kinfolk.

Visitors are welcome to view the totems and to attend dedication ceremonies. Today, more than 80 totems are found throughout the Duncan area; 41 of them can be viewed by following the yellow foot-

You can't just make up a totem pole.
— Norman Tait, Nisga'a pole carver

prints painted on sidewalks. Duncan is on Vancouver Island, 61 km north of Victoria on Highway 1. Information is available from the Duncan Travel Infocentre, 381 TransCanada Highway, Duncan, BC V9L 3R5, (604) 746-4636, fax (604) 746-8222. In summer, guided walking tours of the totems depart regularly from the caboose on Canada Avenue, (604) 748-2133.

A Commemorative Totem: Rick Hansen

Rick Hansen, wheelchair athlete, completed an incredible journey between 1985 and 1987. Under his own power, he completed a 40,081 km journey through 34 countries. His "Man in Motion" world tour raised millions of dollars for spinal cord research. But more importantly, it delivered another sort of message to the able-bodied. "We've got lives and hopes and dreams like everyone else," said Hansen. Inspired by the tenacity of this valiant young man, the native community of Duncan erected a totem to honour Rick's great accomplishment. It can be found near the train station museum.

NATIVE HERITAGE CENTRE: DUNCAN

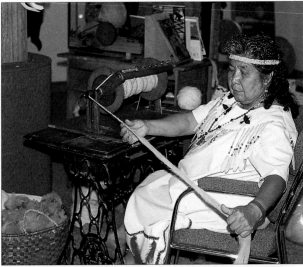

Ruby Peter, a spinner and knitter at the Heritage Centre, can remember when her father first drew the designs that came to be her family's exclusive knitting patterns.

In previous times, the Khowutzun people of the Coast Salish Nation rejoiced because they were blessed to live in this warm and beautiful land. Today, they share their pride with outsiders through their own heritage centre. Visitors have the opportunity to learn about Khowutzun culture and to experience face-to-face visits with the people.

Passing through the front gates, visitors begin at the nah-num, a fire circle where, for generations, all learning begins. The Longhouse Story Centre features a repeating laser-assisted welcome film. The 25-minute presentation was produced under the supervision of tribal elders.

Each of the buildings on the site echoes the traditional architecture of these coastal people. The large Khowutzun Arts and Crafts Gallery is stocked with carvings, masks, cedar baskets, silver jewellry, and books. Sometimes a local knitter or spinner is present to demonstrate her skills. Another longhouse showcases the history of Cowichan-knit sweaters. Well known for their warmth, the genuine articles are produced in limited numbers. Under the roof of a large carving shed, totem poles take shape. Carvers are sometimes present.

The Big House Restaurant was originally constructed for use at Expo '86 in Vancouver. At 464 sq m, it is the largest bighouse on site and was designed by architect Henry Hawthorne. The building was engineered using seven red cedar roof beams, each 21 m long and weighing about 9 t. The roof of the great hall soars to a height of 9 m. The restaurant menu is adapted from traditional Cowichan fare.

At regular intervals each day in summer, a native guide in regalia conducts tours of the centre. He or she explains the day-to-day life of the Cowichan people and answers questions.

Weekly during the summer season, a 4-hour presentation called "Feasts and Legends" is held. The deep booming of drums beckons guests to the banks of the river, where the ceremony begins. After a traditional welcome in *Hulqumenum*, the language of the people, four witnesses are called. Later, these honoured guests will be called to take hold of the talking stick and relate the evening's experience from their own eyes. At the river, the Ceremony of the First Salmon is performed and a fern-draped salmon is presented to the chefs. As part of the six-course feast, outdoor grilled salmon is served with steamed vegetables. After the meal, dancers perform. The audience is encouraged to join the dancers during the Friendship Dance and to dance in the spirit of all those who walk together as friends.

Participation in the "Feasts and Legends" requires an extra fee, so call ahead for times. Information is available from the Native Heritage Centre, 200 Cowichan Way, Duncan, BC V9L 4T8, (604) 746-8119, fax (604) 746-4143.

Tony Charlie, Tour Guide

Tony Charlie is one of the friendly tour guides who work at the Native Heritage Centre. Delivering commentary is the formal part of his job, and occasionally hugging tourists is the informal part. Throughout a regular work-day, Charlie changes his regalia several times. "Sometimes I am in such a hurry, I worry that I might dash out partly dressed," he says charmingly. "At least it would get people to ask questions." Charlie's mother is Kwakwaka'wakw' and his father is Coast Salish, so

Come ... Share Our Pride
—Native Heritage Centre

he has many stories to share. Visitors get more out of their experience if they take the time to strike up a conversation with the staff. "That's what we are here for," Charlie says.

Native Arts: Duncan and Chemainus

Arts of the Swaqwun Gallery, 80 Trunk Road, Duncan.
(604) 746-5000
Bigfoot Indian Trading Post, 5203 Trans Canada Highway, Duncan.
(604) 748-1153
Cherry Point Studio, William Kuhnley, Jr., Nitinat.
(604) 746-4526
Hill's Indian Crafts, 5209 TransCanada Highway, Duncan.
(604) 746-6731
Images of the Circle Studio, 9722 Chemainus Road, Chemainus.
(604) 246-9920
Judy Hill Gallery and Gifts, 109 Craig Street, Duncan.
(604) 746-6663
Ken's Gifts and Crafts, 97765 Chemainus Road, Chemainus.

(604) 246-2422
Khowutzun Gallery, 200 Cowichan Way, Duncan.
(604) 746-8119
Modeste Wools, RR 6, 2615 Modeste Road, Duncan.
(604) 748-8983
Native Heritage Annual Art

Show and Sale – November, Native Heritage Centre, 200 Cowichan Way, Duncan.
(604) 746-8119,
fax (604) 746-4143
Sa-Cinn Native Enterprises, 9756 B&D Willow Street, Chemainus.

Petroglyph Park: Nanaimo

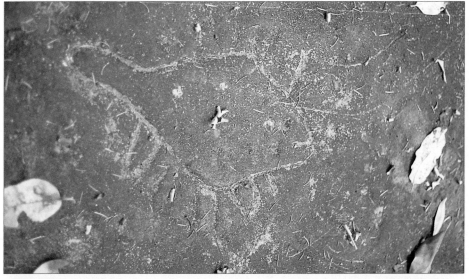

Though the exact meaning or purpose of petroglyphs has been lost to time, the indelibly etched figures speak of the search for harmony between humans and nature, between humans and the divine.

A petroglyph is a figure carved into a rockface, usually near a body of water. Not to be confused with pictograph paintings, petroglyphs are grooved into sandstone or granite. Found everywhere in the world where prehistoric people have lived, each region's style of rock writing is distinctive. Petroglyph sites are protected under legislation in France, Spain, Hawaii, Alaska, Oregon, and British Columbia.

The method of making petroglyphs is known. The mason first pecked out the outlines with a stone hammer. After chipping out small holes, the grooves were abraded into smooth channels.

However, the age and meaning of petroglyphs remains open to conjecture.

Efforts to date them have been uncertain. As to their meaning, there are many theories. Scholars tend to favour religious meanings. Haida elders report they cause rain. The Tlingit people say they are a record of sacrificed slaves. Still other natives scoff at all these claims. They contend the figures are merely doodles, chipped out by weary initiates waiting for a spirit-vision, or by bored paddlers waiting for the tide to change. Whatever the origins, the simple outlines of animals and other-worldly creatures fascinate onlookers.

Individuals can make their

May I have strength of arm; may my arm never get tired—from thee, O Stone !
—Prayer of a Stone Carver, Secwepemc

own petroglyph-rubbings at the Nanaimo Centennial Museum, (604) 753-1821. Petroglyph Park is located 2 km south of Nanaimo on Highway 1. Information is available from the Travel Info-Centre, (604) 754-8474.

Additional petroglyphs are found nearby at Sproat Lake near Port Alberni. Information is available from the Travel Info-Centre (604) 724-6535. Small reproductions of petroglyphs are available in stone from Portfolio West, 1092 Hamilton Street, Vancouver, BC V6B 2R9, (604) 685-6554.

THE EAGLE AERIE GALLERY: TOFINO

An artist rides a wave of dreams to encounter wisdom-spirits, whose voices inspire their next creations. Even when a storm blows in from the nearby ocean, the Eagle Aerie Gallery and its works of art offer a tranquil and snug refuge from the storm.

Impossible to miss in the tiny village of Tofino B.C., the Eagle Aerie bighouse is a distinctive building with copper-panel doors, carved beams, and painted totem poles. It is devoted to the works of Tsimshian native Roy Vickers, an artist noted for his stylistic adaptation of traditional designs and use of brilliant colours. After spending his childhood in the native village of Kitkatla, Vickers trained at the Northwest Coast Native Art School in 'Ksan near New Hazelton. He now runs his own gallery and successful business with the help of his brother, Matt.

Vickers' works have become a hallmark for British Columbia. In 1987, the provincial government presented Her Majesty Queen Elizabeth II with a Vickers' painting titled, *A Meeting of Chiefs*. In 1993, on the occasion of the Vancouver Summit, President Bill Clinton received Vickers' serigraph, *The Homecoming*.

Vickers chooses to live in Tofino to be inspired by the white beaches, crashing waves, everpresent winds, and the annual migration of the gray whales. The public is welcome to visit his gallery and other nearby native-owned galleries.

> *I want people to see my past, my roots, the old ways in my paintings.*
> —Roy Henry Vickers, 1990

Native Arts: Mid-Island

Clinta's Indian Crafts, 7581 B Pacific Rim Highway, Port Alberni
(604) 724-0133

Du Quah Gallery, 1971 Peninsula Street, Ucluelet
(604) 726-7223, fax (604) 726-4403

Eagle Aerie Gallery, 350 Campbell Street, Tofino
(604) 725-3235, 1-800-663-0669, fax (604)725-4466

House of Himwitsa, 346 Campbell Street, Tofino
(604) 725-2017, fax (604)725-2361

Hy'emass House Gallery, 468 Island Highway, Parksville
(604) 248-2423, fax (604) 248-4844

TSA·KWA·LUTEN LODGE: QUADRA ISLAND

Situated in a 445 hectare forest overlooking Discovery Passage, this native-owned resort can accommodate 80 guests in 26 ocean view suites. Four cabins directly on the beach have private verandas and fireplaces. Guest services include a sauna, a small fitness facility, and an outdoor hot tub. Fishing packages are also available.

Native-style food is served. On a cliff overlooking the ocean, whole salmon are stretched onto cedar slats and cooked over an open fire. The restaurant prepares seafood dishes sometimes served in the Great Room. On Fridays, guests are invited to participate in a Kwakwaka'wakw' feast. This may include clam fritters, baked mussels, fiddlehead ferns, salmonberries, dulse, and steamed prawns. After this special dinner, a Kwakwaka'wakw' dance troupe, the Moon Dancers, performs ceremonial dances.

Nearby are the Kwagiulth Museum and stone petroglyphs. Visitors can go beachcombing, visit the Cape Mudge Lighthouse, and watch the infamous dark tidal flows swirl around the island. Many ships have been wrecked offshore. Eagles and ospreys are prevalent and orcas pass by the lodge in season.

Part of a new wave of native-owned tourism businesses now being developed in British Columbia, the Tsa·Kwa·Luten Lodge was

ABOVE: Reminiscent of a traditional bighouse, the main hall of the lodge is used as a multipurpose gathering space and occasionally as a restaurant.
INSET: Moon Dancers perform for guests on Friday evenings.

built by the band on native land after ten years of careful deliberation among the local Kwakwaka'wakw' people.

Information is available from Tsa·Kwa·Luten Lodge, Box 460, Quathiaski Cove, Quadra Island, BC V0P 1N0, (604) 285-2042, 1-800-665-7745, fax (604) 285-2532.

Quadra Island is a 10-minute ferry ride from Campbell River; for info, contact BC Ferries, (604) 286-1412.

KWAGIULTH MUSEUM AND CULTURAL CENTRE: QUADRA ISLAND

ABOVE: Activity programs for schools and visitors bring an added dimension to static displays of museum artifacts. Here, children try on traditional robes.
INSET: The button blanket robe was originally made with abalone shell buttons. Today pearl or plastic buttons are used. The button figure portrayed is the wearer's family coat of arms.

The Kwagiulth Museum displays many items associated with Winter Dances. Not to be confused with potlatches, Winter Dances were originally choreographed by secret societies and went on for many weeks. Monster puppets flew on suspended ropes; hollow tubes threw actor's voices; costumed dancers disappeared through hidden trap doors. Governed by the native-run Nuyumbalees Society, this bighouse museum displays dance paraphernalia, such as headdresses, masks, and costumes. Most items were created by Kwakwaka'wakw' artists.

Prior to the annual Winter Dances, certain young men were abducted and taken to live in the forest. There the dancers fasted alone to prepare for the "Cannibal Bird" drama. Disheveled, hungry, and disguised from head to toe, these dancers suddenly appeared in the darkened bighouse. From the audience, guards rose, shell-rattles in hand. They quickly stood alongside each disoriented dancer. "Hap, hap, eat, eat" the frenzied dancers cried. Their large beaked masks snapped menancingly at the audience. It was rumoured that while they were away, the abductees feasted on corpses. Attempting to mollify their cravings, the guards doused them in oil, choked them with smoke, or gave them food. Eventually the guards' efforts were of no avail

and the spirit-filled dancers set upon the audience. Several people were bitten. The carved wooden skulls hanging from some of the dancers' costumes threatened even more frightening consequences. Women and children who fainted during these long tense performances could be punished.

Photographing some of these dances is prohibited to the present day. Visitors may participate in various activity programs at the museum, such as making petroglyph rubbings. Information is available from the Kwagiulth Museum, Box 8, Cape Mudge Village, Quadra Island, BC V0P 1N0, (604) 285-3733. To reach the island via a 10-minute ferry from Campbell River, contact BC Ferries, (604) 286-1412.

CAMPBELL RIVER MUSEUM

In the past, everyday objects from wooden quivers to berry baskets were richly embellished. The noble class had privileges that were rigidly defined. But it was a sign of the value placed on artistic ability that low-ranking commoners could sometimes gain extra privileges, if their crafts were admired by a chief or elder.

Unfortunately, many of the artifacts which were important to prehistoric artisans were made of wood, reed, bark and hide. These materials do not preserve well—except in unusual circumstances. Studies of surviving material indicate that coastal art developed more than 2,000 years ago.

This museum contains native articles from Vancouver Island. On display is a comprehensive basketry collection and individual artistic works. One series of carvings depicts native perceptions of an undersea world. Among the most noteworthy pieces are masks created by the famous Kwakwaka'wakw' carver, Willie Seaweed.

Situated on three hectares of parkland overlooking Discovery Passage, the museum also sponsors a series of visitor-participation programs and guided tours. Topics may include the native use of plants for medicine.

Information is available from the Campbell River Museum, 1235 Island Highway, Campbell River, BC V9W 2C7, (604) 287-3103, fax (604) 286-0109.

This Nuu-chah-nulth mask was acquired as part of a general collection in the late 1970s (before the present curators- began to keep detailed records). Little is known about its origins. However, there is a class of masks owned by shamans. Only the shaman knows the mask's meaning, and he or she takes that knowledge to the grave.

A Camera Safari: Totem Poles at Campbell River

Eagle pole, Thunderbird pole at Discovery Inn.
Dzunukwa pole at Tyee Plaza Mall.
Thunderbird pole at the Museum.
Carved house posts and Heritage Pavilion at Foreshore Park.
Roberts Suncrest pole at Thunderbird Hall.
Two memorial poles at We-Wai-Kum Band Cemetery.

THE WEST COAST PEOPLE TOUR

Storytelling, crafts, and gourmet food are the highlights of the West Coast People tour.

Since 1974, West Coast Expeditions has offered 6-day educational wilderness adventures on the north coast of Vancouver Island, with departures from Campbell River and Fair Harbour. It is a unique experience for those who seek rapport with the land, the sea, and native people. Up to fifteen participants are accommodated at their well-equipped base camp located on a remote island in Kyuquot Sound. Kyuquot and Checleset natives live nearby on Upwowis, one of the villages within the Nuu-chah-nulth nation.

Some of this wilderness coastline has remained unchanged since the native people first lived here. Ancient totems and bighouse structures slowly being reclaimed by nature speak silent stories of many generations long past. People of the territory continue to celebrate culture and nature with traditional songs, stories, art, and food.

West Coast Expeditions' guests enjoy informal evenings of conversation and traditionally prepared native meals, shared with the Jules family. Locally harvested delicacies, such as fresh halibut, salmon, and Dungeness crab are frequently provided by native people to help furnish the camp's gourmet menu. Native elders help to shape the program by telling stories and demonstrating their skills. Each day, participants venture forth via motor boat to interesting destinations around the island. Marine animals that thrive in the area include sea lions, sea otters, gray and minke whales, orcas, and a variety of marine birds.

Tour leaders, tents, mattresses, and meals are provided and, while rain gear is available, it is advisable to bring personal weatherproof clothing and footwear. Information is available from West Coast Expeditions, 1348 Ottawa Ave, West Vancouver, BC V7T 2H5, (604) 926-1110, 1-800-665-3040, fax (604) 926-1110.

43

U'MISTA CULTURAL CENTRE AND TALL TOTEM: ALERT BAY

The village of Alert Bay has power arising from the secret that generation after generation gathered and performed their most sacred ceremonies when it was illegal to do so.

The Alert Bay Kwakwaka'waka' community now guards the treasures of the old potlatch. Housed in a cultural centre, the U'mista is modelled after a traditional bighouse. The potlatch regalia on display represents the survival of a tradition that was almost lost.

The recent history of the potlatch is imbued with tragedy. In 1884, as part of a new policy to forbid the ceremony, white authorities began to seize items connected to the potlatch. Important masks, rattles, robes, and coppers were removed. After more than 65 years, good sense prevailed, and the confiscated

items were returned. Among the Kwakwaka'waka' people, potlatching never ceased. But it did go underground. In 1951, potlatches became legal once again.

In earlier times, raiding parties from tribes unrelated by language or blood were part of life. Seeking slaves and goods, the raiding party usually attacked at dawn. When the human booty was sorted out, wealthy prisoners were ransomed back. But commoners could expect a miserable existence from then on. From time to time, a captive was reclaimed in a retaliatory raid and regained his or her *umista*. A great celebration was held. *Umista* means a state of being. The translation

is awkward, but is understood as "he or she is" once again.

Alert Bay today boasts one of the world's tallest totem poles. Now surpassed in height by a totem in Victoria, this lofty pole remains significant as a symbol to the people who held fast during the time of the forbidden ceremony.

The Centre will book dance performances for groups of 50 or more. All visitors view two information videos; allow two hours. Information is available from the U'mista Cultural Centre, Box 253, Front Street, Alert Bay, BC V0N 1A0, (604) 974-5403, fax (604) 974-5499. The Alert Bay Library houses some Kwagiulth artifacts and historic photos. Information is available from the Alert Bay

The U'mista Cultural Centre is located on a small island off the east coast of Vancouver Island.

Library and Museum, 199 First St, (604) 974-5721. To reach Alert Bay via a 35-minute ferry from Port McNeill, contact BC Ferries, (604) 956-4533.

The Tradition of the Potlatch

Much misunderstood by outsiders, the largely secular potlatch once served as a fundamental method for redistributing goods among social classes. Gift-giving was a common occurence. For example, betrothals required the giving of gifts, but these paled in comparison to the scale of a potlatch. From one to three times in his lifetime, a chief's reputation rested on giving away everything he owned, except his residence and his privileges. The goodwill his family gained necessitated reciprocation by other chiefs and elders. Wealth continued to circulate.

There were several legal matters attended to during a potlatch. Witnesses were appointed to remember the details of each official act. Those who had performed services or received injuries were publicly compensated. New names were given out, marriages were performed, and survivor's benefits were allocated. All guests

---

I am the first to give you property, tribes. I am your Eagle, tribes!
—*Boasting Chant, Kwawaka'wakw', 1934*

---

were well fed, gifted, and entertained for days on end.

The most significant gift item was copper. Pieces were broken off from a shield-shaped copper plaque and given to high-ranking guests.

The giving of copper was accompanied by a complex set of rules meant to humiliate rival chiefs who were unable to reciprocate with gifts of equivalent value. Before contact, potlatch gifts might include generous numbers of baskets, bentwood boxes, carved masks, large feast dishes, grease ladles and ivory carvings.

After contact, the potlatch became decadent. A single ceremony might involve 200 sewing machines, 50 stoves, 2000 blankets, and 1000 cooking utensils. It is said that missionaries who trained native women to sew were dismayed to find their hard-won sewing machines donated to a potlatch. The native view was different. Whoever received the machine would probably learn to sew too, making the whole society richer.

COPPER MAKER CARVING STUDIO AND GALLERY: FORT RUPERT

Members of the fourth, fifth, and sixth generation Hunt family pose by the river. Each generation can point to esteemed members who have contributed to the continuation of Kwakwaka'wakw' culture.

In 1850, a Hudson's Bay Company employee from Dorsetshire England, settled in a small native village on northern Vancouver Island. Mr. Robert Hunt went on to marry high-ranking Mary Ebbets, the Tlingit daughter of Tongass tribal Chief Shaiks from Alaska. Together, they founded a proud family line. For many years around the turn of the century, their eldest son Robert acted as interpreter and collaborator to early anthropologists Franz Boas, Edward Curtis, and Samuel Barrett. Mrs. Margaret Frank, Robert's great-grandaughter, better known as "Auntie Maggie," is now 100 years old. She once portrayed the beautiful "princess bride" in a sepia tone film screened regularly in many museums today. This 1914 ethnographic drama titled *In the Land of the War Canoes.*

Some years ago, Auntie Maggie split her traditional name, *Ooma-galis.* She bestowed half of it on Gloria Roze, another Hunt descendant, to honour her for teaching traditional dancing to the children and for her excellence in creating blanket robes. Ms. Roze's young dance troupe remains active and is composed of fifth, sixth, and seventh generation Hunt family members.

Presently, Calvin Hunt, the

> *We all have three ears. The third ear is the heart.*
> —Gloria Roze, member of the Hunt clan, 1994

youngest son of the late hereditary Chief Thomas Hunt, along with his wife Marie, operate the Copper Maker, a carving studio and gallery open to the public. Calvin has collaborated with renowned artisans Henry and Tony Hunt. Three other members of the Hunt clan regularly carve at the studio: Tom Hunt, Steven Hunt, and Mervyn Child.

Hunt family works are available through the Copper Maker, 112 Copper Way, Fort Rupert village, 15 minutes south of Port Hardy. Button blanket robes by Gloria Roze are available through the studio. The young Kwakiutl Dance troupe perform each August at Vancouver's Pacific National Exhibition, (604) 542-3707. Information is available from the Copper Maker, Box 755, Port Hardy, BC V0N 2P0, (604) 949-8491. Dancing performances or blankets in the Kwakiutl style are available on commission; please contact (604) 949-9913.

Native Arts: Central and Northern Vancouver Island

Copper Maker Studio, Hunt Family, Port Hardy (Fort Rupert)
(604) 949-8491
Hill's Indian Crafts, 20 Commercial Street, Nanaimo
(604) 248-2423
Hill's Indian Crafts, 1140 Shoppers Row, Campbell River
(604) 287-9946
Island Images, 1015 Tyee Plaza, Campbell River
(604) 287-8911

Robert Hunt

Names and Naming

All right. I am the highest ruler in these parts. I will take the name of King. I will be William King.
—Peguis, an Ojibwa chief whose native name meant "destroyer," on taking a new name at his baptism in 1838.

The naming of an object, a person, or an animal, is an important act among native people. In past traditions, a child might live for a number of years without a "real" name. Among prairie tribes, a young boy was given a silly sounding name, until he earned a dignified one. Native stories contain phrases such as "... and it was then called 'deer'." More power came to an animal once it received its name. To the present day, a white who contributes to a native community might be honoured with a new name.

Native people themselves may receive more than one name in a lifetime. In some groups, it is customary to receive a name from each branch of the grandparent's family, for a total of four names during a lifetime. Names are given out at irregular intervals, sometimes casually, sometimes at a remembrance service. It is considered impolite to utter the names of the deceased individuals, but their names can be passed on. Native people are not always told what their name means. And not all native people will share their native names with outsiders.

TOTEM POLES: STANLEY PARK, VANCOUVER

The poles at Stanley Park are well maintained. Most are duplicates of poles from the Kwakwaka'wakw' tradition. The unpainted pole on the left is a Nisga'a original.

Stanley Park is a 400 hectare forested area in the heart of Vancouver, in part preserved in its original state. The collection of totem poles at Brockton Point represents styles from a few of the northwest Pacific coast native traditions.

Some of the poles recall native stories. For example, the unpainted Nisga'a pole with beaver figures tells of five brothers. Peering into the beaver lodge, they were amazed to see the animals take off their skins and become humans. Subsequent-

ly, the boys begged their chief to stop hunting beaver. On top is Eagle Person holding Raven, and under is a figure holding Frog and Eagle. These represent carver Norman Tait's two sons.

The Thunderbird pole was carved by Kwakwaka'wakw' Tony Hunt. While this is a duplicate, the 1901 original can be spotted in a 1914 Edward Curtis film. Curtis was an early anthropolgist; he travelled through the area documenting natives at contact.

The most photographed pole includes pursed lipped Old-Woman-of-the-Woods. As

visitors pose in the warm embrace of her inviting arms, few realize that she was noted for stealing children.

The Haida box-totem is a mortuary pole. In earlier times, the Moon-face board would have fronted the coffin of a chief. The figure with cloven hooves is Mountain Goat, and Grizzly Bear holds a seal, not a salmon.

The big beaked pole depicts Raven, a trickster figure. Raven's beak is made from an overturned canoe. Carved in 1890 as a memorial to the Wa'kas family, the original once fronted a bighouse in Alert Bay. The original was

also the subject of a painting by artist Emily Carr (Klee Wyck). This duplicate features the human Wise One and Cannibal Bird. It was carved by Kwakwaka'wakw' Doug Cranmer.

In 1880, the native village of Whoi Whoi stood on this site, but a smallpox epidemic spread through the settlement. Alarmed authorities burned the village. In 1889, the park road was paved with tons of crushed clam shells taken from a 2 m deep, 1 km long midden, a shell and refuse dump. About 1900, domesticated buffalo grazed in the park. One sign read: "To Right, Buffaloes; To Left, Big Trees."

Deadman's Island received its name in the 1860s. In early times, native burial boxes were laid to rest high in the trees. About 1890, it was suggested that the little island be logged. The Squamish people who live immediately across the Inlet, protested vigorously until the Vancouver Lumber Company changed its mind.

Siwash Rock offshore of the northwest side of the park is accessible on foot from Second Beach. The Squamish natives call the rock *T'elch*, after a noble who was famous for his charitable ways. The story took place during the time of waiting for the great redeemers. T'elch was an exceptionally kind man. But once he was accused of performing good deeds only so his rewards would be greater than others. T'elch was hurt. He set out to purify himself. While taking a very cold swim in the ocean, he met four men arriving by canoe. Upon hearing of his

Raven was a trickster figure. Here, his beak is constructed from an overturned canoe. On the original pole, the beak opened to reveal a small ceremonial entrance to the house.

humiliation, they revealed themselves to be the redeemers; T'elch was blessed. After his death, he was changed into a stone monolith, where he remains an inspiration for his people.

Stanley Park is located at the north end of Georgia Street. Information is available from the Vancouver Travel InfoCentre, Plaza Level, 200 Burrard Street, Vancouver, BC V6G 3L6, (604) 683-2000, fax (604) 682-6839.

Tekahionwake, Author and Poet

Also known as Pauline Johnson, this Mohawk woman of letters died in 1913 at the height of her fame. Thousands lined the streets for her funeral; and her memorial now stands at Second Beach in Stanley Park. Best known for her works *Flint and Feather*, and *Legends of Vancouver*, she is said to have named the pond in the park. Originally connected to the sea, it would drain at low tide. Once it was altered by park architects, she missed paddling her canoe in her little "Lost Lagoon."

In *Legends of Vancouver* (1911), Tekahionwake said, "There are those who think they pay me a compliment in saying I am just like a white woman. I am an Indian, and my aim, my joy, my pride is to sing the glories of my people."

LYNN CANYON PARK AND WILDERNESS TRAILS: NORTH VANCOUVER

ABOVE: Natives say there is a timeless quality found in the deep forest. Who is to define the difference between the life of a human and the life of a growing thing? Who is to say exactly why a soul became a human instead of a tree? INSET: The Lynn Canyon Suspension Bridge leads walkers into a dramatic forested area once revered by Coast Salish people.

Greater Vancouver lies on the edge of a mountainous wilderness. City visitors can quickly leave the urban environment and explore forested settings. They remain much as they were before contact. Several semi-wilderness day trails are accessible from starting points in North and West Vancouver.

One easily accessible forested setting is Lynn Canyon Park. The forest here was a spiritual place for the Coast Salish people. Echoes of forest spirits flutter silently in the shadows. Dominated by Douglas fir, western and mountain hemlock, and western red cedar, the deep canyonside forest engages the senses. Though the area endured limited logging in 1912, the splendour of the trees so impressed the McTavish brothers, that they ceased logging and donated the land for a park. A suspension footbridge was later built. Hanging 50 metres above Lynn Creek, the span leads left to a short trail through to Thirty-foot Pool. Though the ground surfaces are uneven, the root-bound trail is rated as an easy 40-minute round trip walk; wear suitable footwear.

At the entrance to Lynn Canyon Park, an octagonal building houses the Lynn Canyon Ecology Centre. The staff will screen nature films, explain the displays, and distribute trail maps. During July and August, daily guided nature walks start here.

Prepared hikers and walkers can explore other urban-edge forest areas. Recommended two-hour walks are Capilano Regional Park trail, Yew Lake trail in Cypress Provincial Park, Indian River trail in Mount Seymour Park, and Lighthouse Park trail in West Vancouver. Recommended four to six-hour hikes are Lynn Headwaters Park, the Seymour Demonstration Forest,

Cypress Park, and the Baden–Powell trail system. Trails range from moderate to difficult. Mountain weather can change rapidly and hikers should bring protective clothing, matches, water, and food. Trail maps are compulsory.

Bear warnings, cougar warnings, and additional restrictions may be in effect. Always inquire at Park Headquarters if intending to stay out overnight.

Information is available from the Lynn Canyon Park

Ecology Centre, 3663 Park Road., North Vancouver, BC, (604) 987-5922. Books containing maps of these urban-edge trail systems are listed in the reference section.

Stanley Park

When white explorers first arrived in the area now occupied by the city of Vancouver, there were several Salish villages along the waterfront.

The Salish people lived in impressive cedar houses which hugged the beaches in long rows wherever abundant food and fresh water could be found. People moved about according to the season, often maintaining homes at both summer and winter villages, as well as shelters at various food-gathering camps.

The peninsula located in the centre of this painting was wisely set aside for parkland—an unusual municipal action in 1889. Today, Stanley Park remains a green oasis in the centre of a bustling city. The forests high on the mountains also remain green.

Vancouver: then a remote wilderness, now a thriving city

A Camera Safari: Totem Poles in Vancouver

Two commemorative poles....................Van Dusen Gardens
Expo '86 poles..............................Plaza at 750 Pacific Blvd
Pole collection, indoor, outdoor............Museum of Anthropology, UBC
Tall pole...................................Maritime Museum, Ogden St., Kits
Tait pole on bighouse.......................NEC, 285 E. 5th Ave
Dzunkwa pole................................CBC, 700 Hamilton St
Outdoor pole collection.....................Stanley Park
Hunt pole and carved door panels.......Horsehoe Bay, West Vancouver
Thunderbird pole............................Lynn Canyon Park, North Vancouver
Three Tait poles, indoors..................Capilano Mall, North Vancouver

Additional information is available from the Vancouver Travel Infocentre, (604) 683-2000.

CAPILANO SALMON HATCHERY AND PARK: NORTH VANCOUVER

Featuring glass insets so visitors can witness the fish as they struggle during their final upstream journey, this hatchery is especially noted for its architectural design.

A **staple of the native** diet for thousands of years, salmon were available in seemingly endless supply. After contact, the supply situation changed. Less than 100 years of logging, mining, construction, and frontier population growth have devastated salmon habitats. In 1900, the annual commercial catch was 134 million kg; by the 1930s, it was half of that.

Efforts to increase salmon yields began in earnest in 1977. The federal and provincial governments established the Salmonid Enhancement Program (SEP). Special facili-

ties are now in place to aid the fish while migrating and spawning. Fishway chutes assist the fish past dams and other blockages. Incubation boxes are placed on stream bottoms to assure a continuous supply of fresh water to fertilized eggs. Spawning channels are constructed adjacent to streams to provide oxygenated water for sockeye runs. Rearing ponds, large areas where the fry are fed, protect the young until they can survive in the wild.

Hatcheries are the most common type of enhancement facility. The hatchery staff collect eggs and milt from returning adult fish. After

tending to the rearing process for one to two years, each tiny fish is marked with a nose tag. The young are released. Nosetags help to trace the ocean journey of each fish. Many hatcheries are located in remote areas, and are operated by native bands, an important adjunct to their traditional ways.

The Capilano Hatchery is named after Salish Chief Khahtsahlano of the Burrard band, who lived in the area in the first part of the century. Open to free self-guided tours year-round, a fish ladder, rearing tanks, and live salmon specimens are on display. The rearing tanks are covered with bird-resistant wiring and are teeming with young fish. The species of adults that arrive between late August and October include steelhead (sea trout), coho, and chinook. The facility was built to preserve a salmon run blocked by the Cleveland Dam. In turn, the Cleveland Dam provides a part of the fresh water supply for Greater Vancouver.

In previous times, native people fished with bone barbs, spruce root ropes and floats. After contact, native people saw little reason to change their equipment. In fact, several visiting white captains commented on the great success they experienced when they used the indigenous methods.

To gain an overview of the entire Capilano hatchery facility, cross the river by footbridge, turn right for a fifteen-minute walk to an overlook located in Capilano River Regional Park.

Capilano Hatchery is located west of the sign on Capilano Road, North Vancouver. Information is available from Capilano Hatchery, (604) 666-1790. A map of the Capilano River Regional Park is available from (604) 432-6350. A publication, *Where and When to See Salmon*, is available from Fisheries and Oceans Publications, #400, 555 West Hastings Street, Vancouver, BC V6B 5G3, (604) 666-0384.

A Native View of the Animate and Inanimate

Along the Pacific northwest coast, the cycle of life and death is vividly apparent. The salmon migration in the animal world corresponds roughly to a fallen cedar log in the plant world. Both natural cycles illustrate that new life springs from life passing away.

It is not surprising that coastal native philosophy reflects an easy transition, not only between living and non-living forms, but between all life forms: animals, plants, and humans. Raven becomes human; Elderberry and Stone argue about who will give birth first; rocks in the sea grow up to be inhabited islands; a grieving mother visits her son's body and finds a bright young man.

In the Squamish tongue "Atcine! Atcine! Atcine! Kwinay-atcsi its tem kwina-si-all-i" means, "Oh dear! Oh my! We have been told that a handsome young man lies below. Oh that he would come up." This life-view translates into a reverence for all living and non-living earthly forms, separated by only a thin veneer.

NATIVE CUISINE: VANCOUVER

ABOVE: Consisting of delicious bounty from the land and the sea, traditional native foods like the Potlatch Platter (shown here) are now adapted to contemporary tastes.
INSET: Bonnie Thorne is the owner of the Quilicum Restraunt. One of Bonnie's Nuu-chah-nulth names is Yes'ta.

Pacific coast natives have always enjoyed a bounty of food from the land and the sea. From ancient times to the present, mountain goat, deer, beaver, ducks, geese, grouse, salt and fresh water fish continue as regular menu items. The seashore provides a variety of clams and oysters, sea urchins, crabs, and octopus. Sea lion and sea otter were hunted in previous times; occasionally, disabled whales washed up on-shore. The oolichan smelt-fish provided a tasty dipping sauce; its fatty grease or "butter" was a profitable trade good.

There were several traditional cooking procedures. Water was brought to a boil by adding hot rocks to water-tight boxes. There were several methods of baking in earth-ovens and cooking over open fires. Foods were sun-dried, then wrapped in birchbark and preserved in earth cellars. If predators were a problem, off-the-ground caches were built. Heavy-laden berry patches were controlled by specific families who traded dried berries for other goods. One type of berry, the soapberry, whips up into a stiff egg white-like foam and though exceptionally tart, was considered a treat. After contact, natives quickly learned to make delicious forms of bannock—a type of lightly fried bread. Today, it is argued they make bannock better than anyone else.

Traditional native foods have now been adapted for modern tastes. The Quilicum Restaurant is operated by Nuu-chah-nulth natives Bonnie Thorne and her partner, artist Art Bolton. Thorne's special preparations of local

A rich man is coming to the banquet. Keep your real feelings silent.
—Old Chant of the Wolf Clan

seafood and wild meats attract a wide following and much praise. The Potlatch Platter—a succulent feast of marinated caribou, prawns, oysters, barbecued salmon, and Alaska black cod is served on carved wooden dishes. Volumes of guest books attest to the worldwide patronage this unique little eatery has attracted.

"Once a man arrived at the airport straight from Germany, begged for a seat at the restaurant—because he had no reservation—and after sharing a table with some gracious customers, he immediately flew back to Germany. He appeared to be a satisfied and happy man." Thorne says.

Information is available from the Quilicum Restaurant, 1724 Davie Street, Vancouver, BC V6G 1W2, (604) 681-7044. The native-owned Gathering Place Café, 3010 Sleil-Waututh Road, North Vancouver, (604) 929-9408 specializes in buffalo burgers. A native-owned catering service specializes in moose stew and native foods; contact Just Like Grandma's Bannock, Dolly Watts, (604)

An Outdoor Dinner with the Squamish People

During the winter months, the Squamish area near Vancouver is home to more than 3000 Bald Eagles, the largest documented population in North America. A dinner-tour with native people takes in this sight in season or allows visitors to appreciate other wildlife. Participants first embark on ocean kayaks for a two-hour flatwater paddle through the serene estuary. As the group lands, people from the Squamish Nation wait on

255-2243, fax (604) 255-7866. The Salmon House on the Hill, 2229 Folkstone Way, West Vancouver, (604) 926-3212 is

the river bank. Salmon is roasting on the fire. After dinner, one of the native elders tells stories. This year-round experience is also available without the kayak component; minimum group size is 10. "Many of our seniors are kayaking for the first time," says the owner. Information is available from Everything Outdoors Ltd, Box 415, Brakendale/Squamish, BC V0N 1H0, (604) 898-4199.

reputed to serve the finest barbequed salmon in Vancouver.

Native Theme Tourist Attractions:North Vancouver

Grouse Mountain: Titled "Our Spirit Soars," The Theatre in the Sky presents a 30-minute multimedia video exploring a native carver's transformation from a mortal into a bald eagle. The laser-assisted production repeats at regular intervals. You reach the top of Grouse Mountain by aerial tramway. Information is available from the Theatre in the Sky, 6400 Nancy Greene Way at the summit of Capilano Road, North Vancouver, BC, (604) 984-6619.

Capilano Suspension Bridge: The oldest tourist attraction in Greater Vancouver. In 1889, Scotsman George Mackay built the bridge with the help of two local natives, August Jack Khahtsahlano and his brother Willie. The Coast Salish first called it the "laughing bridge" because its ropes whistled in the wind. In 1993, Nancy Stibbard, the present owner, commissioned a totem pole to honour elder Mary Khahtsahlano. Well into her late

90s, Mary crossed the suspension bridge to walk in the forest.

Today, visitors can cross a new 137 m span swinging 70 m over the Capilano River and visit a tiny forested park. Native carvers periodically work on site. Salmon barbeques are scheduled in summer. Information is available from the Capilano Suspension Bridge and Park, 3735 Capilano Road, North Vancouver, BC, (604) 985-7474.

MUSEUMS: VANCOUVER AND AREA

Situated beside the ocean at the University of British Columbia, the Museum of Anthropology houses artifacts collected from several aboriginal cultures, with a special emphasis on totem poles. Inside the soaring Great Hall are mortuary poles, house posts, and carved house entrances. Giant Woodpecker, the story of a great flood, and the penetrating eyes of Haida spirit-figures are depicted among the towering giants. Also on display are rare potlatch objects: ladles, baskets, bent boxes, and enormous feast dishes. In the backrooms, the Museum's research collection reveals Winter Dance transformation masks, examples of Haida argillite, and one potlatch copper, the embodiment of a chief's wealth. Ceremonial objects in silver, gold, argillite, bone, and wood are displayed in elegant cases. For the museum's contemporary collection, Haida artist Bill Reid was commissioned to produce a cedar sculpture, *Raven and the First Men*. Women enter the scene later in the story. Raven features prominently in the creation myths of Bill Reid's people.

Outside the museum, visitors can view three bighouses. Villages with up to 50 of these buildings

The proud glory of the People of the Salmon is rekindled through presentations of their artifacts, both beautiful and rare.

were common along the coast. Several outdoor totems, each created by a famous totem carver, are positioned about the grounds. With the snow-capped mountains in the background, it is easy to appreciate the fullness of the native civilization that has resided here for thousands of years.

The front doors and exterior wall panels were created by

> *I call these poles my silent teachers.*
> —Norman Tait, Nisga'a pole carver

Tsimshian carvers. Visitors can stand in the footsteps of US President Bill Clinton and Russian Premier Boris Yeltsin, who posed here under a Kwakwaka'wakw' Portal during the 1993 Vancouver Summit.

A second major collection is displayed at the Vancouver Museum at Vanier Park in Kitsilano. This collection emphasizes the Coast Salish people who remain on the lands now occupied by metropolitan Vancouver. One display shows that prehistoric people in this area practised trepanning, that is, boring a hole in the skull to release

pressure. In the more recent past, the Salish were famous for their woven rain hats. Examples of Chilkat blankets, fishing equipment, cedar clothing, and talking sticks are on display. A full sized Nuu-chah-nulth canoe, once used for whale hunting, looms among related harpoons and whaling equipment. Several important potlatch coppers

hang inconspicuously in plain display cases. This museum also sponsors transient exhibitions of masks and native art.

Another Vancouver museums of interest is the Simon Fraser Museum of Ethnology, which houses a collection amassed from B.C. archaeological digs.

Included in the collection are a number of musical

instruments, a selection of carved serving dishes, numerous bent wood boxes and many examples of houseposts and totem poles. This small, student-run museum emphasizes the archaeological approach to native culture. Diagrams indicate how researchers map out a site, and photographs document how skilled stone knappers chip and shape flakes of basalt and obsidian into tools, arrow heads and other cutting implements.

The Museum of Medicine houses a medical collection of objects and plants used by native people. The Vancouver Art Gallery owns and displays a number of paintings by artist Emily Carr.

Information is available from the UBC Museum of Anthropology, 6393 N.W. Marine Drive, Vancouver, (604) 228-3825, free on Tuesdays; the Vancouver Museum, 1100 Chestnut Street, Vancouver, (604) 736-4431, free to seniors on Mondays; the Simon Fraser Museum of Ethnology, Department of Archaeology, Simon Fraser University, Burnaby (604) 291-3325; the Museum of Medicine, (604) 736-5551; and the Vancouver Art Gallery, (604) 682-5621.

Form Follows Function

Built in the shape of a Coast Salish hat, the Vancouver Museum is an architectural tribute to the people who occupied these lands before contact. Known as the "People of the Tall Grasses," the Coast Salish were famous for their tightly woven hats. During the rainy season, the sloping hats proved water-resistant. In the sun, they provided shade. Shown here, the typical hat is worn by **Twance** (inset photo above), a Kwak-waka'wakw' dancer from the Vancouver Island village of Fort Rupert.

NATIVE ARTS IN VANCOUVER

The art of the Pacific northwest people reflects an interconnectedness between human experience, animal realms, and dream worlds. Ceremonial masks are one illustration of this link. Some are known as transformation masks. They are constructed to open up, revealing a second face inside. For example, a Greed Mask might feature a benevolent face outside and an avaricious face hidden inside. Certain masks are so heavy they require shoulder supports, a protective head cap, and a

By the light of the dwindling fire, actors peek through spaces in the mask's mouth, nose, beak, or neck. This lack of eyeholes allows the mask's artist to concentrate great expression in the eye area.

Modern Potlatch Woman

"I go on my tastes and the market."
—Patti Rivard, Nuu-chah-nulth, 1993

When **Patti Rivard** first opened the Wickanninish Gallery, she decided to specialize in native-made silver jewellery and a few select craft pieces. If she considers the design to be excellent, she will sell it. "Artists come to me by word of mouth. I tend to go with up-and-coming native artists because their prices are a bit better, but they know the pieces they show me must meet with my high design criteria," she says.

Born in Tofino, near the crashing waves of the open Pacific, Patti spent her childhood admiring the beadwork and

weavings that her grandmother created. As an adult, she started one of the first native-run businesses in Vancouver. Ms. Rivard was awarded the Top Performance Award of the Vancouver Business Association in 1993. During the last seven years, as thanksgiving for her good fortune, she has given two traditional potlatches for her people back home. "I might have to give a third one," she adds. Information is available from the Wickanninish Gallery, 1666 Johnston Street on Granville Island, Vancouver, (604) 681-1057.

stick strapped in the back and secured around the waist of the wearer for stability.

Guardian spirits are everywhere. Canoe makers are watched over by Woodpecker, anglers by Salmon, hunters by Wolf, and shamans by mystical beings. In early times, when a young man went on a vision quest, his revelations took on an animal form.

Aboriginal artists combine their knowledge of the spirit world with their expertise in graphic techniques. The resulting art enjoys a reputation as being among the finest indigenous art forms in the world. Popular media among B.C. native artists include silver and gold, transformed

A necklace crafted in shimmering silver makes one think of moonbeams, cool and radiant. It portrays the mighty Thunderbird, a magical lustre combined with a shimmering glow.

into jewellery; cedar and birch, carved into masks; ivory from extinct mammoths or whale

teeth, formed into ornaments. Mammoth tusks are found regularly in the Northwest Territories. Some of the best known B.C. native art forms are engraved silver bracelets and distinctive red and black screened print designs.

Recently, native-designed fashion clothing has become popular. Tribal crests and variations of crests are appliquéed onto robes, tams, skirts, capes, and jackets. Native-design clothing is available through Betty Ann Pennier and Jill Fisk, Legends Alive, (604) 732-4429; or Dorothy Grant, Feastwear Enterprises, (604) 538-3585.

Native Art: Greater Vancouver

All My Relations Bookstore, 2025 West 4th Ave, Vancouver (604) 739-2144

Art Bolton Jewellery and Carvings, 1724 Davie Street, Vancouver (604) 681-7044

Canoe Pass Gallery, #115, 3866 Bayview Ave, Steveston (604) 929-4673

Chief's Mask Bookstore, 73 Water Street, Vancouver (604) 687-4100

Cowichan Knits and Crafts, 424 West 3rd Street, North Vancouver (604) 988-4735

First People's Art, #102, 12 Water Street, Vancouver (604) 662-7845

Gallery of Tribal Art, 2329 Granville Street, Vancouver (604) 732-4555

Granville Native Art, 2241 Granville Street, Vancouver (604) 731-7719

Heritage Canada, 356 Water Street or 650 West

Georgia, Vancouver (604) 669-6375

Hill's Indian Crafts, Gastown, 165 Water Street, Vancouver (604) 685-4249

Images for a Canadian Heritage, 164 Water Street, Vancouver (604) 685-7046

Inuit Gallery, Gastown, 345 Water Street, Vancouver (604) 688-7323

JAAM Native Arts, 650 West 41st Avenue, Vancouver (604) 266-7891

Khot-La-Cha Handicrafts, 270 Whonoak Street, North Vancouver (604) 988-1930

Leona Lattimer Gallery, 1590 West 2nd Ave, Vancouver (604) 732-4556

Marion Scott Gallery of the Arts, 671 Howe Street or 801 West Georgia, Vancouver (604) 685-1934

Museum of Anthropology Gift Shop, 6393 NW Marine Drive,

UBC Vancouver (604) 822-5087

Potlatch Arts, 100, 8161 Main Street, Vancouver (604) 321-5888

Richard De La Mare Jewellery, 2257 Dollarton Highway, North Vancouver (604) 272-0095

Sea Hawk Auctions, 3243 264th Street, Aldergrove (604) 657-2072

The Indian Gallery, 456 West Cordova Street, Vancouver (604) 684-6290

The Trading Post, 3735 Capilano Road, North Vancouver (604) 985-7474

Vancouver Museum Gift Shop, 1100 Chestnut Street, Vancouver (604) 736-5417

Wayne Eustache Carving Tradeworks, 520 Powell Street, Vancouver (604) 873-3775

Wickanninish Gallery, 1666 Johnstone Street, Vancouver (604) 681-1057

WHERE NATIVES GATHER: VANCOUVER

ABOVE: Children from the Squamish Nation impatiently await their turn to dance at a totem pole raising in North Vancouver. INSET: Native elders help prepare salmon for the large crowds at a festival. The fires burn from early in the morning until late at night.

In past times, extensive dance ceremonies took place during the winter months. With the larders full, there was time for feasting, and dramatic story-telling. Winter Dance ceremonies were first choreographed by secret societies. Each year they competed among themselves for more spectacular special effects. Actors threw their voices by means of kelp tubes; trap doors aided disappearances; puppets flew on strings.

Today, the season for festivals is summertime. But the element of competition is still part of the excitement. Powwows begin with a grand entrance followed by hours of dance competitions. Canoe races pit neighbouring bands against each other on the water. The athletic canoe team members attract quite a following among the young crowd. Baseball tournaments and Sports Days are regular parts of the band's annual events.

A unique feature of Pacific coast festivals is the native version of fast food. This often consists of bannock or fried bread-on-a-stick, and barbecued salmon. Prepared on alder slats over an open fire, fresh salmon takes on a delicate smoke flavour. Elders take turns tending the fires and cooking large quantities of salmon snacks for the public.

Public Native Events: Vancouver and area

Whey-AH-Wichen Canoe Festival, North Vancouver ....May
Squamish Nation Canoe Races, North Vancouver.........................July
Squamish Nation Powwow, North Vancouver...............................July

The Aboriginal Pavilion at the Pacific National Exhibition in Vancouver sponsors a series of native demonstrations and a craft show in August and early September, (604) 542-3707.

Information is available from the Vancouver Indian Centre Society, 1607 East Hastings St, Vancouver, BC V5L 1S7, (604) 251-4844, fax (604) 251-1986.

WEAVER CREEK SPAWNING CHANNEL: FRASER VALLEY

ABOVE: The Weaver Creek spawning channel winds for 13 km.
INSET: The fish are inspected before they enter the channels.

water oxygenated and cool. Fish ladders aid the upstream-swimming adults. In the offseason, a special machine is used to vacuum debris from the gravel.

Spawning channels are open to the public. Phone to be sure the sockeye have arrived, usually mid-October. Weaver Creek is east of Vancouver, near Harrison Lake. From the Lougheed Highway, turn north on Morris Valley Road; after 300 m, take the right fork and follow the signs for 13 km. Information is available from Fisheries and Oceans Canada, (604) 666-0384; or the Travel InfoCentre, (604) 876-3088. Along the route, the Chehalis Band Hatchery is also open for visitors. Information is available from the Chehalis Indian Band, (604) 796-9846.

ockeye salmon have the reddest flesh of all salmon species. This makes them desirable both for chefs who wish to impress their restaurant patrons and for canning, because their flesh retains a vibrant colour in the tin.

When salmonid enhancement programs first begin, it was discovered that this sought–after species could not be propagated in hatcheries. The first technical response was to upgrade the natural streambeds where the sockeye return. Stream water was filtered to clear it of particulates. Small waterfalls were improved so the tumbling water would be well oxygenated. Bottom gravel was filtered to remove large rocks. Although these measures were effective, they could not

prevent floods. In an unusually rainy year, such a deluge might wipe out much of a sockeye run.

To solve this problem, huge holding-tanks were constructed to contain floods. Additionally, to encourage active spawning, miles of specially designed winding S-channels and water gates were built. Small waterfalls and rows of shade trees keep the

Large Spawning Channels

Adams River, near Chase ....October
(dominant runs 1994,1998, 2002)
Babine Lake, off Hwy 16, w of Prince George..September annually
Seton Creek, near Lillooet.....................................October in odd years
Weaver Creek, near Harrison Hot Springs...............October annually

Information is available from BC Travel InfoCentres: Adams River (604) 372-7770; Babine Lake (604) 847-5227; Seton Creek, (604) 392-2226, 1-800-663-5885; Weaver Creek, (604) 876-3088.

HATZIC ROCK: MISSION

Offerings are placed around the base of Hatzic Rock to revitalize the spirits that lay dormant within. The rock can then begin to dispense its protection once again.

Situated on an otherwise unremarkable site is a huge, half-buried boulder called Hatzic Rock. A glacial erratic left by a receding glacier some 30,000 years ago, it is a solitary reminder of the power of natural forces. Distinctive features, such as this one, were often chosen as landmarks by ancient people. Sto:Lo elders have long told a story about this particular rock. They say a seditious man was turned into a rock as punishment for his disobedience. Frozen into stone, he watched forlornly over his community.

In 1989, during the construction of a new subdivision, bulldozers accidentally unearthed several native artifacts. The Sto:Lo people were called in, and they consulted anthropologists at the University of British Columbia. The accidental unearthing of artifacts near this rock confirmed stories that the Sto:Lo people had long reported. Hatzic Rock had guarded an active community.

After a year, a major dig was funded and the outlines of prehistoric houses and firepits were uncovered. Each litre of excavated soil was put through a seive. Simple tools and flakes of sharp rock were recovered. Minute fragments were collected and are still being separated from the soil. By extrapolating the food consumed from discasrded shells,, the number of prehistoric people who lived here can be estimated.

An interesting process has since begun. The Sto:Lo are "re-activating" the rock. Offerings are brought to the site and ceremonies are held near it. During 1994, it is slated to become a tourist attraction under the direction of the band. On the site is an interpretive centre explaining the dig and the story behind the community that once thrived here.

Hatzic Rock is located 2 km east of Mission. Information is available from the Mission Travel InfoCentre, (604) 826-6914; or from the Indian Friendship Centre, 33150A First Ave, Mission, BC V2V 1G4, (604) 826-1281, fax (604) 826-4056.

WHERE NATIVES GATHER: FRASER VALLEY

The powwow is said to represent a celebration of the survival and adaptation of native culture. Always non-commercial in nature, powwows attract spectators with nothing more than word-of-mouth advertising. An audience outside the local community is neither cultivated nor expected. However, some outsiders always manage to find their way to these events. The dances that are performed are witness to a surviving lifestyle first developed among the ancient people on this continent. Native music and dancing are increasingly shared across tribal boundaries and between many traditions. During a powwow, each dancer has the opportunity to give physical expression to the experience of being native.

Native Arts: Fraser Valley

Bigfoot Moccasin Factory,
Suite 3, 2009 Abbotsford
Way, Abbotsford
(604) 854-8380

Muskwa Gallery and Sto:lo Native Handicrafts,
773 Water Ave, Hope
(604) 869-5000

Peter's Arts and Crafts,
Exit 151, Peters Road, Hope
(604) 794-7059

Seabird Island Café and Giftshop,
77 Haig Highway, Agassiz
(604) 796-9852

Photographed at the Seabird Island Annual Canoe Races in Agassiz, thirteen-year-old Cori-Marie Sandy is a Princess of the *Merritt Miss Conayt Friendship Society*.

Public Native Events: Fraser Valley

Seabird Island Indian Festival, Agassiz .... May
Cultus Lake Indian Festival, Cultus Lake .... June
John Pennier Memorial Canoe Races, Agassiz .... July
International Powwow, Mission .... July
Annual Stein Festival, Lytton-Mt.Currie .... August

Information is available from the Mission Indian Friendship Centre, 33150 A First Ave, Mission, BC V2V 1G4, (604) 826-1281, fax (604) 826-4056.

THE SECHELT NATION: SUNSHINE COAST

The unique group of figures at Sechelt is sometimes called the "Stonehenge" grouping. Across all times, in all native cultures, the circle symbolizes equality, safety within bounds, and the inclusion of all.

In 1986, this Coast Salish native band became an independent self-governing body. The Sechelt Indian Government District now holds jurisdiction over its lands and uses its authority to provide services for its residents. Among its holdings are gravel operations and its own airline, Tyee Air. Backed by an RCMP officer who is also a Sechelt elder, and with the help of aboriginal medicine women, the band also runs a healing centre at Jervis Inlet. Using traditional methods, including the sweat lodge, the centre rehabilitates troubled native youth from across British Columbia.

A Stonehenge-like group of carved figures symbolizes these accomplishments. Standing on a grassy bank on their traditional lands by the sea, some figures have no faces. These represent the Band's previous position. Other figures are carved with the Eagle crest and forward-looking faces. These represent the present and the future.

There are a number of facilities and events for visitors to attend at the Sechelt Cultural Complex in Sechelt. Located at the side of the main highway, the House of Héwhíwus or the "house of chiefs," includes a small basketry museum and a native-owned craft store. The Raven's Cry Theatre, a 270-seat facility, periodically presents native storytellers. Sechelt Nation

Canoe Races and dances are held from time to time. The nearby Sechelt Band Hatchery [(604) 885-5562] is open to the public. Tyee Air is available for charter (604) 681-5678, (604) 525-2411. For further information, contact the Sechelt Cultural Complex (604) 885-2273, or the Tsain-Ko Gift Shop (604) 885-4592. To get there by road from Vancouver, there is 40-minute ferry crossing from Horseshoe Bay to Langdale, then a 30-minute drive on a paved road. Contact BC Ferries Information, (604) 685-1021, (604) 886-2242.

SKOOKUMCHUCK REVERSING RAPIDS: SUNSHINE COAST

When the tide is not in transition, Skookumchuck Narrows is a calm inlet. However, twice a day, the tide changes and incoming water surges through the narrows to meet the outflowing river.

Due to a peculiarity of geography, the Skookumchuck Rapids occur when the tide is forced to reverse on itself. On the incoming tide, ocean waters rush into the confines of the inlet and build up on one side. On the outward flow, the buildup reverses and rushes through the narrows. During these times, boiling cauldrons, whirlpools, and swirling eddies are evident. The difference in water levels between one side of the rapids and the opposite end sometimes exceeds two meters. The speed of the changing current has been clocked at more than 30 kph. On a three-meter tide, more than 440 billion litres of water churn through the channel.

Skookumchuck means "strong turbulent waters."
—Coast Salish

Native people held this place in great awe and respected its power. There are several pictographs in the area.

To find the time of a tide change during daylight hours, contact the Travel InfoCentre, (604) 885-3100. To get to the Sunshine Coast from Vancouver, there is a 40-minute ferry crossing from Horseshoe Bay to Langdale. Contact BC Ferries (604) 685-1021, (604) 886-2242. To get to Skookumchuck Narrows Provincial Park, travel north on Highway 101 past Sechelt and Pender Harbour, turn right at the Egmont turn off, 1 km south of Earls Cove, and follow the signs to a parking area. To get to the Rapids, walk 4 km along the trail past Brown Lake. There are direc-

tional signs and restrooms along the route. The easy trail meanders through lush coastal forest; there are few elevation changes. The estimated walking time is one hour. Those who dare to view the rapids from the water, may contact Tzoonie Charters (604) 885-9802, (604) 885-9053.

Native Arts: Sunshine Coast

House of héwhíwus Gift Shop, 5555 Highway 101, Sechelt (604) 885-4592

Powell River Historical Museum, Willingdon Park, Powell River (604) 485-2220. This museum carries a collection of native baskets.

Texem-ay Crafts, 69, 7100 Alberni Street, Powell River (604) 485-2060

Tsoonie Native Crafts, 5644 Cowrie Street, Sechelt (604) 885-9802, (604) 885-9053

TSOONIE OUTDOOR ADVENTURES: SUNSHINE COAST

This native-owned tour company's mini-adventure is a five-hour cruise and salmon cookout. Skirting the tidal rapids of Skookumchuck Narrows, the charter boat *Tsoonie* passes native pictographs, fish and oyster farms, then docks at a remote recreation area. While visitors wait for their salmon luncheon, there is time to go exploring in the bush.

For those seeking a longer outdoor living experience, the company also offers various boat-access overnight camping adventures. In addition to supplying the usual tent, mattresses, and cooking utensils, the company provides a canoe, fishing gear, a crab trap, and a clam rake.

The experience of the wilderness can be invigorating. After a hard day of watching herons or trying to catch crabs, visitors may enjoy a pleasant soak in the hot tub located in the wilderness. Lying back in the steaming waters, it is not unusual to spot mountain goats on the surrounding cliffs or watch airborne eagles fighting over their catch. There are hot showers in the woods nearby.

Aleta Giroux and her husband Art run this adventure company. Their aim is to help people make a quick transition from urban living to camping comfortably in the wilderness. Aleta, a Plains Cree by birth, says, "We are easy to find and easy to take."

ABOVE: As the eagles swoop overhead, visitors enjoy a relaxing soak. INSET: Aleta Giroux

Before contact, novice shamans would take to the woods to seek out their dreams. Women, as well as men, could become shamans. In settings such as these along Narrows Inlet, they performed fasts and learned how power might come to them through spirits. Among the Coast Salish people, this power could be obtained by seeking a vision from a guardian spirit. After a cold-water bath at dawn, appropriate rituals, and the experience of isolation in the wilderness, the seeker approached the frame of mind needed to receive a meaningful song. From an early age, children were encouraged to find their own special song.

Today along the Sunshine Coast, visitors can enjoy seal-watching, aquatic birds, and seek peacefulness in the surrounding forest. Some visitors are able to perceive the powers felt by the Salish people and their shamans — not so long ago.

Information is available from Tsoonie Outdoor Adventures, Box 157, 5644 Cowrie Street, Sechelt, BC V0N 3A0, (604) 885-9802, (604) 885-9053. To get to the Sunshine Coast take a 40-minute ferry ride from Horseshoe Bay to Langdale, then 30 minutes by paved road. Contact BC Ferries, (604) 685-1021.

TRADITIONAL FISHING AREA: LILLOOET

To the present day, the Lil'wat people gather at certain places along the Fraser River to catch salmon and dry them on racks. During the height of the run in July and August, they assemble on the river banks. The hot winds that blow through this section of the canyon provide excellent conditions for drying salmon. With temperatures reaching as high as 40°C, the area acts as a natural furnace. The Lil'wat people were once important intermediaries in the lucrative salmon trade business between Coastal and Interior native groups.

Today, only tribal fishermen are allowed to place permanent nets along the Fraser River. Anchored to the shore, and employing a boom, the net swings from its moorings into the current. It is swung back to retrieve the fish. In other locations, young native fishing experts stand on the rocks. Using spears, they gaff silvery fish from the swift-running waters. On the riverbank, women clean the fish, then split them into a characteristic shape. The heads and tails are discarded and the sliced bodies are hung on horizontal poles. Occasionally, a tarp is thrown over the poles and a slow cottonwood fire imparts a smoky flavour to the fish. In the old days, the entire fish was used, its dried skin toasted over a fire, and fish-eye soup was highly prized. For a treat, fresh fish dipped into oolichan butter are eaten raw.

The Fraser River supports an active native fishery. Approximately 80 percent of all the salmon on the west coast of North America migrate up the Fraser and its tributaries. If Salmon Beings were treated with respect, native people believe their spirits return to an underwater Salmon House, acquire new bodies, and make the run again.

According to tradition, the first salmon taken at each important fishing site was considered the leader, whose command the other fish obeyed. This first fish was given special attention. Carried like an honoured guest to an altar and sprinkled with red clay dust, speeches were made to it. It was cooked in a ritual way. All participants ate from it. Most importantly, its bones were put back into the water so they could return to the underwater village where salmon reside. Thus, in subsequent years, a reincarnated Salmon would come back and bring its followers.

Outsiders may observe native fishing activities as they occur today. Do not interfere with the fishers or the drying racks. If spending time among the people, a gift of food is appropriate. Ask permission before photographing individuals, including children. This is a traditional area and

natives have the right to carry on without acknowledging visitors or being disturbed.

The Lil'wat fishing camp is located under the Old Bridge in Lillooet. It is occupied in season, usually July and August. Information is available from the Friendship Centre Society, Box 1270, Lillooet, BC V8G 2N7, (604) 256-4146, fax (604) 256-7928. The annual Lillooet Indian Band Powwow is open to the public and takes place in May. Information is available from (604) 256-7357.

Six Villages of Totems: Hazelton Area

For centuries, the area around Hazelton has been the home of the Gitksan and Wet'suwet'en peoples. Today, many visitors take time to travel to a series of six neighbouring native villages, each of which is the site of a group of fine totem poles. Some of these totems are the oldest still standing in coastal BC. The native people in this region are conscientious about preserving their totems and keeping them unaffected by fads.

Each village displays a number of poles. Kispiox means "place of hiding." There, on the base of one pole, is a figure of Ya-el, the founder of the village. On a nearby pole is the base figure of Weeping Woman. She holds a grouse that was captured too late to save her starving brother. On top is One-Horned-Mountain-Goat, the pole-owner's family crest. Another pole displays the Grizzly-Bear-of-the-Sun family crest, topped by White Owl, another family crest. One of the oldest poles, thought to have been constructed in the 1860s, features a tiny ceremonial entrance-hole surrounded with human-like figures.

At Hazelton Village, at the foot of Government Street, a pole carved about 1889 was relocated here from the village of Gitanmaax. It displays several frogs, probably representing the Flying Frog family crest. One figure, Bushman, is gently cupping a frog in

The poles of the Nass River tribes...among the finest... in existence.
—Maruis Bareau, ethnologist, National Museum of Canada, 1927

the same way a shaman holds a patient's soul in his hands.

At Kitwancool, one totem figure holds a child sucking its hand, the only known totem figure so touchingly portrayed. Here also is Giant Woodpecker, a helpful spirit with many of the same powers as Thunderbird.

Nearby, at Kitwanga, is the Kitwanga Fort National Historic Site, a place of totems and the location of Battle Hill. An area map is available from the Travel InfoCentre, Box 340, Highways 16 and 37, New Hazelton District, BC V0J 2J0, (604) 842-6571, fax (604) 842-6077.

How Old are Totem Poles?

Totem poles are generally constructed from untreated cedar logs. Though cedar is resistant to insects and fungi, the effect of weathering is relentless. After 70 to 100 years battling the elements, totem poles tend to decay and fall over. An old totem is the responsibility of the descendants of the family that erected it. Until that family can afford to commission a duplicate, the spent totem may lie on the ground. It has not been forgotten. When arrangements are completed, family carvers are appointed. The old pole is carefully moved to a carving shed, such as the one pictured, and a duplicate is made. If there are no talented carvers in the owner's clan, outsiders may be appointed. However, in that case, an appointed family member must "stand over" the hired carvers during every moment of the process. In the end, the re-carved pole becomes a symbol of honour for the family.

A Camera Safari: Hazelton Area

Hazelton..1889 pole
Kispiox, north of Hazelton..............................Poles and hatchery
Gitsegukla, near Skeena Crossing...................................Poles
Gitwangak, just off Highway 16 on north side of Skeena............Poles
Kitwanga, near Battle Hill..Poles
Kitwancool, on Highway 37................................Old poles, shed

KITWANGA FORT NATIONAL HISTORIC SITE: KITWANGA

ABOVE: Tall grasses atop a secluded windswept hill are all that remain of the famous Battle Hill. **INSET:** Signs on site explain the fort's former elaborate defenses.

Battle Hill Fort (Ta'awdzep) was built by the Gitwangak people near an important river trade route alongside the Skeena River. Its beginnings have been lost in time, but the fort's demise was marked by a fiery battle in the early 1800s.

Many people think of fort in a frontier, military, or fur-trading context. But native people in this region built forts for several reasons: to defend their territory, to exact compensation for crimes against them, to collect tolls from passers-by, and to further the aims of their secret societies.

This fort, known on maps and signs as Battle Hill, was constructed on top of a glacial mound overlooking the river. It was surrounded with palisades, and featured an ingenuous system of stacked logs secured with cedar ropes that could be released to roll down onto enemies, crushing them. Troups of armed warriors were permanently headquartered on-site. In battle, they wore armour made of leather and slate pieces or tough grizzly bear hide, plus fearsome wooden helmets and face-guards. An elaborate system of whistle signals made up the warning system. When visitors approached, a sentry blew coded signals from whistles held in both hands. Visitors were expected to approach, then stop and wait quietly—in full view, until the next signal. Any deviation from this routine was considered treachery.

The most famous warrior to occupy this fort was a man known as Nekt. His descen-dants continue to live in the native villages of the area. Several modern clan crests have developed from the legends of his life. One group of descendants displays the Grizzly from which Nekt made his armour. Another has adopted the crest of an Eagle medzek (armour) that he captured during a raid on the Kitimats. A third group has adopted a symbol representing the spiked logs of the fort.

On maps and signs, Kitwanga Fort National Historic Site is also called Battle Hill . There are interpre-tive signs and trails on the site. Unsuitable for wheelchairs, there are many steps. To get access to the site from High-way 16, take Highway 37 north from Kitwanga; travel past Gitwangak about 8 km. The site is near the native village of Kitwancool. Nearby is archael-ogical evidence of pithouses, food cache pits, and a sweat house. Information is available from the Travel InfoCentre, Box 340, Highway 16 and 37, New Hazelton District, BC V0J 2J0, (604) 842-6571, fax (604) 842-6077.

'KSAN NATIVE VILLAGE: HAZELTON AREA

As visitors stroll through this re-created village, the colourful past peeks out at every turn. Brightly painted doors on plain cedar plankhouses speak of traditions forged in the long ago. Numerous totem poles are located within a 50-km radius.

Near 'Ksan village at Hagwilet canyon, the Skeena River passes through a natural trap. Migrating salmon were forced through a few narrow openings where native people placed basket-traps. With an abundant supply of food and natural protection from enemies, the village prospered.

'Ksan, located at Gitanmaax, is the replica of a native village that echoes those that have stood at this place for centuries. Today, seven decorated tribal houses fronted with several totems stand silently on the banks of the Skeena and Bulkley rivers. There is no charge to wander around, but visitors are encouraged to take the guided tour, both to learn more about the people and to enter three buildings that are normally locked: the Frog House of the Distant Past, the Wolf House of Feasts, and the Fireweed House of Masks and Robes. The Frog House features items that were part of everyday life before contact. The Wolf House depicts the changes that came about with the advance of white technology. It is furnished as it would be moments before the start of a 1920s potlatch. The Fireweed House contains contemporary masks and robes belonging to the 'Ksan Performing Arts Group.

Also on site are two longhouses open to all visitors. One contains a museum collection and an art gallery,

> *Our crests, our poles, our blankets, our land, That's our mark. Big witness for everybody. All over the world.*
> —Gitksan and Wet'suwet'en Tribal Council, 1991

the other is a gift store. The remaining longhouses are part of an advanced school for native artists and carvers, and are occasionally open for demonstrations.

Once a week in summer, 'Ksan's Performing Arts Group puts on an evening dance performance titled, "The Breath of Our Grandfathers;" phone for times. Guided tours start every hour in summer at the 'Ksan Shop. Information is available from the 'Ksan Indian Village, Box 326, Hazelton, BC V0J 1Y0, (604) 842-5544, fax (604) 842-6533.

Nisga'a Memorial Lava Bed Provincial Park: New Aiyansh

Only 250 years ago, this volcano's deep throat blasted black phlegm into an adjacent riverbed, displacing its clear waters with sulphurous, bubbling, deadly lava and killing many villagers.

Jointly managed by the Nisga'a Tribal Council and BC Parks, this newly created 18,000 hectare provincial park in the Nass Valley has special significance to native people. About 250 years ago, during Canada's most recent lava flow, T'aam Baxhl Mihl Mountain erupted and destroyed two native villages, along with an estimated 2000 Nisga'a ancestors.

According to local stories, the catastrophe was caused by children who inserted rolls of flaming bark into the backs of salmon to watch them swimming around the river at night. Despite the elders' warnings,

other children continued to play this way and ridicule the salmon. One day, the ground began to rumble ominously. A scout was sent to investigate and, upon reaching the top of a mountain, he saw flames and hot rocks raining down. Frantically, he ran to warn the villagers. There was no time to make amends. Some were able to escape to nearby mountain tops, but others, who canoed to the far side of the river, were trapped. As they watched and prayed, a fiery being emerged and blocked the eruption. The supernatural being Gwa Xts'a-gat was so enormous that using only his oversized nose he stopped the flow. Gwa Xts'agat lives within the

volcanic cone today. Children are gently warned never again to make fun of salmon.

Visitors to the park can drive 65 km north of Terrace alongside beds of black lava that follow an old creek bed to the Nass River. Needle-sharp projections, *pahoehoe*, or ropy lava, and *aa* or clinkery lava, underground lava tubes, and small pools of turquoise water dot the eerie landscape. Though two centuries have passed, no plant life has yet returned to the area.

There is a well-marked 8 km walk from the roadside to the crater. A small campsite has been established within the park and there is a picnic area with wheelchair access.

Native Arts: Cariboo, Yellowhead, and Haida Gwaii

Angelique Levac ©92

Adams House of Silver, Masset, Haida Gwaii
(604) 626-3215

Haida Arts and Jewellery, House J6, Old Masset, Haida Gwaii
(604) 626-5560

House of Sim-O-Ghets, Highway 16 West, Terrace
(604) 638-1629

Indian Trading Post, Indian Reserve, Highway 5A, Quilchena
(604) 378-4538

Nak'azdii Handi Craft Shop, Kwah Road, Fort St. James
(604)996-7368

Native Arts and Crafts Shop, 99 South Third Ave, Williams Lake
(604) 398-6831

North Country Arts and Crafts, McBride Timber Road, Prince George
(604) 560-5485

Prince George Native Art Gallery, 144 George St, Prince George
(604) 564-3003

Ras Fine Arts, Hagwuilget Reserve, Highway 62, New Hazelton
(604) 842-6754

Rainbows Gallery, 3215 - 3rd Ave, Queen Charlotte City, Haida Gwaii
(604) 559-8420

The Hiding Place, RR 1, Kispiox
(604) 842-6181

Wet'Suwet'En Arts and Crafts, 1090 Main Street, Smithers
(604) 847-5225

There are no hotels in the immediate area. Grizzly and black bears are frequent visitors to the park, especially to the creeks during salmon spawning season; please obey all posted warnings. At Vetter Falls, visitors can stand on the viewpoint and try to glimpse the phantom fish said to inhabit the falls.

Three native villages in the area welcome visitors: New Aiyansh, Gitwinsihlkw (Canyon City), and Greenville. At New Aiyansh, the school yard displays a tall totem called Unity Rainbow-Man. Gitwinsihlkw residents refer to themselves as the "People of the Lizard," perhaps because lizards are said to pass through fire unscathed. Their interesting village is accessible by a foot bridge. In the Gitwinsihlkw village centre, a new Norman Tait pole symbolizes the people. It is an outstanding work of art. Greeville is a typical modern native village.

Nisga'a Memorial Lava Bed Provincial Park is 100 km north of Terrace on Hwy 152, a partially paved, partially gravel road. In summer the park can be reached by driving 84 km on paved Hwy 37 from Kitwanga, then going west for another 50-some km on a one-lane restricted forestry road. Car insurance may not cover damage that occurs along restricted roads; check before departing and be on the alert for logging trucks. Information on the park is available from BC Parks, Skeena District, Smithers,(604) 847-7320.

HARBOUR BOAT TOUR: PRINCE RUPERT

ABOVE: Hundreds of offshore islands once housed native communities. Visitors can travel among the islands on a charter boat operated by the Metlakatla Band.
INSET: Not in life but in death, this ancestor's precious native identity breaks through. Native art rendered in marble is rare.

At the remote island-village of Metlakatla, a marble grave marker is all that remains to mark a harsh story of domination. In the 1860s, a Christian missionary attempted to remake this native community into a god-fearing utopia by burning all vestiges of aboriginal culture. One native woman was allowed her death wish, delivered with an odd twist. She was allowed to design her grave stone in the "old way." But rather than allow her family to "regress" into their traditional ways while carving it, the design was contracted out to a tombstone maker in Victoria. Today, it is one of the rare examples of BC native art rendered in marble.

A three-hour native-run boat tour leaves Prince Rupert's harbour daily in summer. Visitors travel past evidence of more than 10,000 years of human history. David Archer, tour leader and anthropologist, explains the area. The tour stops at the historic fishing village of Dodge Cove and at the all-native village of Metlakatla. The Prince Rupert area has the highest concentration of archaeological sites in North America and more than 20,000 shell middens within the harbour area. By calculating the weight of the shells and the known amount of meat those shells provided, estimates can be made of the population that the area supported.

Tour start times and tickets are available through the Museum of Northern British Columbia, please see box.

Museum of Northern British Columbia: Prince Rupert

The Tsimshian people continue to live hereabout on hundreds of offshore islands. At the museum, representative Tsimshian cedar objects, ropes, and baskets are complemented by periodic showings of early film footage. Behind the museum is a shed where native carvers occasionally work. A map detailing a "Totem Pole Walking Tour" is available from the Museum of Northern British Columbia, Box 669, 100 1st Ave East, Prince Rupert, BC V8J 3S1, (604) 624-3207, fax (604) 627-8009.

SITES TO VISIT BY LAND: HAIDA GWAII

Clustered off the BC mainland, 150 rain-soaked islands form an archipelago—roughly in the shape of a broken tusk. Though they are known on maps as the Queen Charlotte Islands, the Haida people would prefer them to be called *Haida Gwaii* — "islands of the people."

There are several points of interest for curiosity seekers. An old Haida canoe is located near Port Clements. Only partially hewn, the canoe was abandoned in the forest. The longhouse at Skidegate specializes in Haida art and jewellery; ask for a map of native artists' private homes. Guests may drop in to purchase Haida art. Queen Charlotte Island Museum, Second Beach, Skidegate is dedicated to Haida artifacts and argillite pieces. The Skidegate Band Salmon Project is a Haida-operated hatchery open to visitors. At the village of Masset, on the north end of Graham Island, is the Delkatla Wildlife Sanctuary. This small sanctuary (300 hectares) supports a major wintering bird population and is a critical stopover on the Pacific Flyway during the spring and fall migrations of millions of birds. It also supports a major salmon nursery.

Plants and wildlife that evolve on island archipelagos are unique, and often exhibit subtle, but noticeable differences on each island. Here, as in its famous counterpart in South America, this phenome-

A rare material found only in Haida Gwaii, black argillite is fashioned into sculptures much prized by collectors.

non has been noted. In fact, Haida Gwaii is sometime referred to as the "Galapagos of North America."

In summer, accommodation reservations are compulsory in Prince Rupert and on the islands. Reservations are available through Discover British Columbia, 1-800-663-6000, (604) 387-6371, fax (604) 356-8246. A brochure is available for C$6.00 from the Queen Charlotte Islands Chamber of Commerce, Box 420, Port Clements, BC V0T 1R0, (604) 559-4742. The Singaay L'aa Days at Skidegate are held in June, (604) 559-4496. Getting to the islands from Prince Rupert requires a 7-hour ferry crossing; reservations are compulsory. Contact BC Ferries, (604) 669-1211, fax (604) 381-5452. There is also air service.

The Man From Heaven

Here, a mythic man in stone comes to life. Once, long ago, a stranger sauntered into a bighouse village. Ignoring the totems and refusing to identify his own clan, he nonetheless began to eat their food. The elders were offended. They held a council meeting and ordered his death. "You cannot kill me," he boasted, "I have fallen from heaven." The elders did not believe him. So he took them to a fen beside the ocean. "This is where I fell." The full size outline of his body, indented into rock, was clear for all to see. He

remained with them and was treated with reverence.

This model of the petroglyph is found in the museum in Prince Rupert.

SITES TO VISIT BY WATER: HAIDA GWAII

Skungwaii, more commonly known as Ninstints, is an abandoned Haida village, now in ruins. Located on remote Anthony Island, at the southern tip of South Moresby Island (Gwaii Haanas) in the Queen Charlotte Islands, Skungwaii is approximately 95 nautical miles from the nearest community. The site is designated a UNESCO World Heritage Site. Once home to an ancient Eagle clan, the decaying ruins loom in the frequent mists. Seven heritage sites, longhouses, middens, and more than two dozen totem poles at various angles speak of a people long departed. The thriving Haida community there was wiped out by conflict with early fur traders and disease epidemics more than a century ago. Adjacent to the site is an ecological reserve teeming with seals, petrels, puffins, and other seabird colonies. A number of abandoned Haida villages are accessible on smaller islands. Tanu, another ruin, is a 40 nautical mile journey; Skedans is an abandoned village near a sea lion rookery. In Juan Perez Sound on Hotspring Island, natural steaming springs are accessible to modern-day mariners, about 65 nautical miles distant.

For centuries, the Haida people were considered the greatest of native mariners. Feared for their periodic raids on other groups, in turn they closely guarded their mean-

Ninstints is an abandoned Haida village. Accessible only by water, all visitors must leave the area by nightfall.

dering coastline. Called the "Watchmen," fearless and vigilant, they remain as sentinels against the invasions of restless seas, deep rainforests, and overzealous visitors. There are Haida people who are paid to perform these duties in remote areas of their island homeland.

Visitors who take to the seas should check with knowledgeable mariners or the Coast Guard before setting

out, (604) 559-8383. The sites remain under the guard of the centuries old Haida Gwaii Watchmen. Permits from the Council of the Haida Nation are required before visiting the sites; information is available from (604) 559-4468. Many outsiders choose to visit with an escorted tour. The weather is frequently rainy and cold, even in summer. In an emergency, one must survive in the wilderness.

BY AIR

Vancouver Island Helicopter, Box 333, Sandspit BC V0T 1T0, (604) 637-5344, fax (604) 637-2223; by helicopter, 1-day to 7-day guided flightseeing.

BY LAND

Delkatla Bay Birding Tours, Box 187, Masset, BC V0T 1M0, (604) 626-5015; on foot, birding with a leader; also pelagic tours.

BY WATER

Adventure Canada, 4340 Strathcona Road, North Vancouver, BC V7G 1G3, (604) 929-7375, fax (604) 929-7375; by 65′ sailing vessel.

Bluewater Adventures, 202, 1656 Duranleau St, Vancouver, BC V6H 3S4, (604) 684-4575, fax (604) 689-5926; by stateroom ketch, the 65′ *Island Roamer* for a maximum of 16 guests.

Canadian Outback Adventure Co., 206-1110 Hamilton St, Vancouver, BC V6B 2S2, (604) 688-7206, 1-800-565-8732, fax (604) 688-7290; by 65′ stateroom ketch, customized itinerary.

EcoSummer Expeditions, 1516 Duranleau St, Vancouver, BC V6H 3S4, (604) 669-7741, 1-800-688-8605, fax (604) 669-3244; by kayak, groups with leaders, or aboard the 57′ *Morgaler.*

Haid Gwaii Watchmen Native-Operated Tours, Box 609, Skidegate, BC, V0T 1S0, (604) 559-8225; by special arrange-

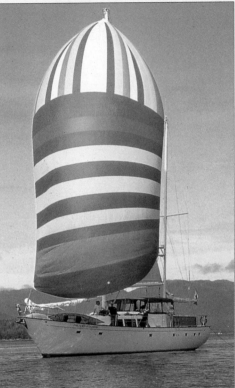

Canadian Outback is one tour company that offers sailing tours among the numerous island of Haida Gwaii. Spotting whales and watching seabirds, along with the spectacle of abandoned native villages, make the experience memorable.

ment only, aboard the *Loo Tass Wave Eater,* 50 ′dugout canoe, a paddling expedition with native guides.

Kallahin Expeditions and Travel Services Ltd., Box 96, Queen Charlotte City, BC V0T 1S0, (604) 559-8455, (604) 5559-4746, fax: (604) 559-8430; full service travel company offering accommodations, car rental,

day-tours by boat, flightseeing by floatplane or helicopter, wilderness overnight boat tours, kayak rentals, sports fishing arrangements.

Kwuna Point Charters, Box 184, Sandspit, BC V0T 1T0, (604) 637-2261, (604) 559-4246; by boat, marine charters with or without escorts.

Moresby Explorers, Box 109, Sandspit, BC V0T 1T0, (604) 637-2215; by kayak, small groups with leader, or kayak rental.

North South Expeditions, 1159 West Broadway, Vancouver, BC V6H 1G1, (604) 726-7447, fax (604) 736-6513; by the *Ocean Vision,* a wooden sailboat, unstructured program.

Northwest Marine Adventures, Box 135, Sandspit, BC V0T 1T0, (604) 637-5440; by boat, hourly or overnight.

SeaKayak Tours, 3218 West 31st Ave, Vancouver, BC V6L 2A7 (604) 264-1668; by kayak with leader, no more than 5 in a group.

South Moresby Charters, Box 174, Queen Charlotte Islands, B.C V0T 1S0, (604) 559-8383; by boat, 4 days with a guide, VHS video of the journey; also vessels for hourly or weekly lease.

The environment of the interior is notable for its large lakes, navigable rivers, forests, and intermittent desert-like areas. The native people here still respect the abundance provided by their ancestral homelands. Winters are short and summers are characterized by periods of high temperatures.

N atives from the land-locked regions immediately east of the Pacific coast, displayed distinctive cultures that reflect the skills gained from living along rivers and lakes. They are also noted for distributing a wide variety of goods up and down the coast and across the mountains to the prairies.

These Interior Salish tribal groups were mainly fishers and gatherers, then hunters. Proficient at harvesting salmon, they also hunted with bows and arrows or dug pitfalls to trap deer, elk, moose, and bear. They strung nets between two canoes to snare waterfowl. The interior groups were also a major source of two types of stone. Steatite, a type of soapstone, was sought after for carving pipes. Hard green nephrite, also known as jade, was made into sharp adze blades.

Despite their close trading ties with other groups, the interior groups did not adopt the coastal class system, totem poles, or teepees. Instead, each band recognized the authority of a hereditary chief and council of elders. Hunting territories belonged to the band as a whole, though some fishing spots and berry-picking areas belonged to specific families. Paintings on boulders or cliff faces (pictographs) have shamanistic overtones and are particularly common

FAMILIAR NAME	ALTERNATE NEW NAMES
Kootenai, Kutenai, Kootenay	Ktunaxa or Kinbasket
Thompson	Nl'akapamux or Ntlakyapamuk
Shuswap	Secwepemc
Lillooet	Lil'wat
Interior Salish	Halkomelem

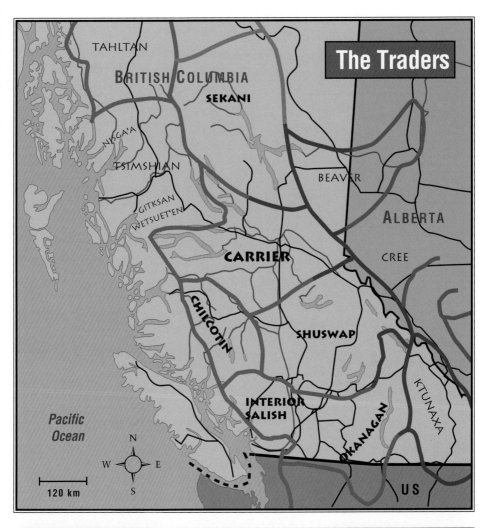

The Traders

TAHLTAN

BRITISH COLUMBIA

SEKANI

NISGA'A

TSIMSHIAN

GITKSAN
WETSUET'EN

BEAVER

ALBERTA

CARRIER

CREE

CHILCOTIN

SHUSWAP

Pacific
Ocean

INTERIOR
SALISH

OKANAGAN

KTUNAXA

N
W—E
S

120 km

US

Chief of the Little Shuswap

Beginning in 1979, Chief Felix Arnouse set up consultations with his people to devise strategies to alleviate their unemployment problems. Re-elected to the position of chief of the Little Shuswap for the last 16 years, his consultations have borne fruit. One major project, the Quaaout Lodge, opened in 1992. "I feel good about the resort," he says, "and the elders are gradually getting used to so many people coming and going on band lands." Local band members also provide game and traditional foods for the Lodge restaurant.

79

DWELLING TYPE: THE KEKULI OR PITHOUSE

A layer of cedar shavings awaits a final cover of earth in this almost completed pithouse. In the winter, a blanket of snow provides an additional insulating layer.

Pithouse depressions and structures are found throughout BC's Southern Interior, most notably in the dry, desert-like environments of the Thompson Plateau and Okanagan Basin. Similar structures have been examined in prehistoric digs in Europe and Asia. During winter months, the Interior Salish people also occupied circular kekulis or pithouses, large bun-shaped houses with sub-terranean floors. Whether the dwelling evolved from those of their Asian ancestors or developed independently, is not known. Archaeologists indicate that as long ago as 3000 years ancient Shuswap people lived in winter pithouse villages consisting of as many as 20 of these large structures.

Each pithouse took up to three winters to construct. First, a hole about 6-12 m in diameter and 1 m deep was dug into the ground. Notched brace logs were angled into the hole to support four rafters. These were tied with willow withes or rawhide. Side rafters were added outside the main rafters. Four heavy timbers framed the top entrance. A separate women's and elder's entrance was built at ground level. The framed structure was covered with poles, then insulated with a layer of sod, wood shavings, and pine needles. Finally, the conical structure was covered with earth. Houses would last for about 40 to 50 winters.

Tiny kekuli structures were built for girls to use for up to six seasons during their initiation into womanhood. Similiarly, during her "woman's cycle," she would reside in this hut. Probably appreciative of the break in routine, she was not allowed to cook during that

ABOVE: Men entered from the top; women and elders had a ground floor entrance. A cover was fashioned to block the top opening on especially cold days.
INSET: The frame of a pithouse is lashed together with leather thongs and cedar ropes.

time. Before returning to the main house, she used a sweat lodge, then bathed, and returned to the main kekuli rested and refreshed.

In summer, the people moved out of the deep pithouses and spent time in conical lodges more like wigwams covered with mats. Since this was the time to fish, snare waterfowl, hunt deer, conduct trade, and travel, this was a convenient and portable structure. But when autumn winds began to blow and the kokanee salmon began to run, the time of the *pelzaluxten* or "going in time" came around and the people returned to the pithouses.

In other interior regions, the dwellings varied. Farther to the north, the Carrier built rectangular winter houses of cedar slabs. Gabled roofs that slanted down to the ground were covered with spruce bark. The homes of the Tahltan tribes were double lean-tos made of poles. Like two open tents facing each other, the bark-covered lean-tos were long enough to house several families.

ABOVE: Climbing on the wooden understructure of a pit house
INSET: Pithouse structure as diagramed by a BC Government Interpretive sign

A Camera Safari: Pithouses in B.C.

Information is available from BC Parks, Thompson River District Office, 1265 Dalhousie Drive, Kamloops, BC V2C 5Z5, (604) 828-4494; or Secwepemc Native Heritage Park, 345 Yellowhead Highway, Kamloops, BC V2H 1H1, (604) 828-9801, fax (604) 372-1127.

THE SWEAT LODGE

Sweat lodges are often located at spiritual places. Inside the lodge, the soft beating of a drum in the sweltering darkness becomes ever more comforting as it picks up the heartbeat of the group.

The custom of taking a steam bath in a sweat lodge is prevalent among native groups from Mexico northward. For the people of BC's interior, however, the sweat is of particular significance.

To the present day, earth-covered sweat lodges are built to various specifications. In the past, the framework of willow branches was traditionally covered with matting and insulated with dirt, bark, and grass. Today, plastic tarps are used to aid the steam-retention qualities of the hut. The entrance is low, so people have to stoop. Participants sit on mats or rags on the ground. Beside the hut is a bonfire circle, where water is heated in blackened pots. Lava-stones are heated and reused. In some traditions, participants must be careful not to step on the heating-rocks, even when they are not in use.

The sweat lodge is constructed in a particularly scenic area, usually near a stream or river. After a group has endured each of four steam phases, they plunge into cold water for a swim. Men usually sweat first, woman traditionally sweat separately. Today, there are mixed sweats.

Undergoing a sweat is a means of cleansing the body

Oh! Oh! Sweat Lodge, take pity on me. Let me live to be old. Help me. Give me the power so I can kill deer.
— Okanagan tribes

and, in previous times, was an important medical practise for the cure of disease. Sweats have a spiritual element. Some sweats are half-day social affairs; others are heavily ritualistic and require a period of preparatory fasting. First, the participants ask the spirit of the sweat lodge to heal them. The sweat ends with a prayer for health and thanksgiving.

In the case of ritual sweats, participants are isolated with a shaman at a secret location for a considerable period. As the rocks glow red in the darkness and the comforting smell of sage wafts through the lodge, elaborate rituals are observed. The ribs of the lodge are named; the lodge is a womb; the grandfather rocks may speak. Significant sweats are advised to help survivors get over grief after the death of a loved one and in the treatment of people with drug and alcohol abuse problems.

Chief Felix Arnouse of the

These Ghost Bells hang in a museum. Commonly associated with solemn sweats among prairie people, the spirits tinkle the bells to announce that a person is "free."

Little Shuswap tells a humourous story. Recently, three Maori natives visiting from New Zealand agreed to take a sweat. When Arnouse sent the boys to cool off in the lake, they did not return.

Anxiously, he went out to look for them. They were standing on the bank trying to decide if the water harboured alligators!

Arrange to Participate in a Sweat

Non-native visitors may arrange to take a sweat. Bookings and arrangements must be made three to five weeks in advance; ask about rates. It must be remembered that a sweat has spiritual overtones. No photography is ever allowed inside the lodge.

• Information on taking a sweat with the Little Shuswap people is available from Chief Felix Arnouse, c/o Quaaout Lodge, Box 1215, Chase, BC V0E 1M0, (604) 679-3090, fax (604) 679-3039.

• Information on taking a sweat with the Coast Salish people and others is available from Noel Blakley, c/o All My Relations Bookstore, 2025 West 4th Ave, Vancouver, BC V6J 1N3, (604) 739-2144.

Deer are abundant in the interior and native people made good use of them. Deer hunters would disguise themselves in a deerskin robe, with a deerhead hat and antlers. Except among the Ktunaxa people, who preferred moosehide, all other groups made garments out of buckskin. Women wore shorter leggings and long skirts. The woman pictured is wearing a traditional Shuswap buckskin outfit with legggings.

Deerskin moccasins made of soft buckskin the colour of a prized pony are manufactured today by the Okanagan Band. Information is available from the Moccasin Factory, Shannon Lake Road, Westbank, BC, (604) 768-3552. The factory is open to the public by appointment.

Sen'Klip Native Theatre and Eco-Tours: The Okanagan

In the summertime in Vernon, the Sen'Klip Native Theatre Company puts on twice-a-week evening performances. Acting in much the same fashion as traditional storytellers, the players recreate the antics of Coyote, mischevious trickster and teacher from the animal world. The Sen'Klip Company's goal is to involve their audience in the visual imagery that remains part of native life.

As the summer sun sets and paints the landscape in shades of gold, the outdoor play begins. Old crippled Owl Woman may introduce the characters. Mother Earth is alive. Crazy Coyote interacts with Deer Woman or tries, unsuccessfully, to outsmart Magpie. Perhaps a thief steals Coyote's eyes when he is not looking. The audience laughs and applauds. The shadows of evening deepen. The plot becomes more complex.

In 1992, the Sen'Klip Company additionally became involved in a tourism industry partnership. Participants can now become involved in the earth-centred traditions of native people during a one-week guided tour. In the company of native guides, visitors experience horseback riding, traditional foods, native teas, canoeing by torchlight, traditional hide-tanning, visits with native artists, songs of the people, traditional flute music and drums, and salmon barbeques followed by

Sen'Klip Theatre actors portray a variety of figures, from Coyote to Deer. These characters originate from a time long ago when animals had human form. In some native cultures, there are Deer Dances. The players bolt for the forest but are captured by the women. Any dancer not captured by sunset is transformed into a real deer.

evening stories. By the warm flicker of the fading firelight, the environment begins to feel as familiar and comfortable as an old friend. These activities represent an exceptional opportunity for outsiders, and they assist indigenous people to maintain their lifestyle on their own tribal lands.

These native-led tour packages have attracted much attention. In September 1992,

the World Congress on Adventure Travel and Tourism showcased the tour. In 1993, the group participated in two tourism conferences in Brazil and Norway. In 1994, they were invited to Germany to explain their program.

The one-week tour or the two-hour plays are both open to the public. Additionally, three-hour native arts and crafts seminars can be arranged for groups of twelve or more. Sen'Klip's home theatre is located at Newport Beach RV Park, Westside Road, 1.6 km north of Vernon; regular performances are held on Saturdays and Sundays in July and August. Information can be obtained from Sen'Klip Native Theatre Company office, 2902 - 29th Ave, Vernon, BC V1T 1Y7, (604) 542-1247, fax (604) 542-3707; or fully escorted tours through the Ecotourism Group, Box 7, Salmon Arm, BC V1E 4N2, (604) 838-7587, 1-800-267-8946, fax (604) 832-6874.

Toom:tem means Earthwoman, our mother who provides all life. Sen'Klip means coyote, from the time when animals had human form.
— Okanagan Shuswap

Public Native Events: The Okanagan Region

Cathedral Lakes Day Celebration, Ashnola...May
Annual Okanagan Native Gathering, Vernon...July
Salmon Barbeque and Dancing, Kelowna...July

Information is available from the Ashnola Band (604) 499-5528, the Westbank Band (604) 760-5666, the Okanangan Tribal Council (604) 769-6455, the Okanangan Friendship Society (604) 763-4905.

A Pocket Desert Reserve: Osoyoos

Now protected as a provincial ecologial reserve, the Pocket Desert records the lowest rainfall in BC. Plants and animals rarely seen in Canada are found within this small, arid strip of land: antelope bush, burrowing owls, turkey vultures, and rattlesnakes are just a few desert species protected in this reserve.

When settlers came into the region only 100 years ago, they set about to irrigate the valley.

However, the land was originally much drier. The sandy portion of the desert is located on the Inkameep Indian Reserve. Native-owned cattle roam the reserve, to the detriment of the plant life.

The pocket desert is found in two adjacent locations on the northside of Lake Osoyoos, 7.5 km north of Osoyoos. Removal of wildlife and vegetation is prohibited. Ask at the Travel InfoCentre for the best way to enter the

ecologial reserve portion of the desert; no permission is required. **Stay on the trails.** Permission is required to explore the sand dune portion of the desert and must be obtained from the band office. Information is available from the Travel InfoCentre, (604) 495-7142, fax (604) 495-6161. For permission from the Osoyoos Indian Band Office, call (604) 498-4906.

SECWEPEMC NATIVE HERITAGE PARK: KAMLOOPS

Located on the Kamloops Indian Reserve on the banks of the South Thompson River, this outdoor cultural experience allows visitors to take a self-guided tour of traditional Shuswap life. The site is located on the remnants of an ancient village, estimated to be 1200 to 2000 years old. The reconstructed full scale Shuswap village includes two summer lodges and four full-sized winter kekuli houses. A walkway leads visitors down to the side of the river and eventually into an old residential school, now used as a museum. Along the path, informative signs explain the land, the way the natives used it, and the customs of the people.

Various implements and utensils from interior native life are shown in their proper setting. Near the river, fishing implements and a salmon-fishing station are on display. Fish weirs were the most effective method of catching the greatest number of fish with the least amount of effort.

In summer, guided tours of the facility are available. The tour leader explains the roles of the women and men, and the uses of various tools. The gift shop carries moccasins,

Fish weirs are stacked up to use in the nearby river. As visitors walk through this park, laughing music sometimes sweeps through on the wind. Like a warming song, it welcomes strangers to the ancestral home of the Shuswap people.

birchbark baskets, pineneedle baskets, buckskin items, beaded earrings, quilled earrings, beaded hair barettes, and a good selection of books.

Events such as salmon barbeques and native songs, dances, and storytelling presentations are scheduled; phone for times. Information is available from Secwepemc Native Heritage Park,

345 Yellowhead Highway, Kamloops, BC V2H 1H1, (604) 828-9801, fax (604) 372-1127. An interesting native art gallery located nearby is the Four Corners Native Art Gallery, 119 Palm Street, Kamloops, BC V2B 8J7, (604) 376-0550, fax (604) 372-1127.

Public Native Events: Kamloops and Area

Annual International Skwlax Powwow, Chase	July
Little Britches Rodeo, Kamloops	July
Annual Traditional Native Feast, Kamloops	August
Traditional Native Sports Games, Kamloops	August
Kamloopa Indian Days, Kamloops	August

Information is available from the Skwlax Powwow (604) 376-3203, or from the Interior Indian Friend- ship Society, 125 Palm Street, Kamloops, BC V2B 8J7, (604) 376-1296, fax (604) 376-2275.

WHERE NATIVES GATHER: KAMLOOPS

Vacationers motoring through Kamloops cannot help but notice the stately old brick buildings perched on a bluff overlooking the South Thompson River. Formerly the Kamloops Indian Residential School and its playing fields, the property has been re-named the Chief Louis Centre in honour of one of the band's most prominent leaders.

In 1993, a large log stadium was built on the school site. It is the new home of the Kamloopa Indian Days Powwow. The 17 bands of the Shuswap invite thousands of native participants, as well as the public, to attend the annual event. During the three days of festivities, the stadium vibrates to scores of native drum groups and hundreds of dancers who arrive from aross Canada and the United States. Dances, accompanied by chants and drums, are among the most ancient expressions of success in the hunt.

At 1:00 p.m. each celebration day, the Grand Entrance begins. Up to 600 dancers in full regalia enter the parade grounds in costumed groups according to their specialty. The dog dancers strut in their spherical feather head-dresses. The war dancers in black and white face stand out boldly against delicate lady dancers in shawls and jingle dresses. Each dance has a history and an associated society.

Even when the powwow drums are silent and the chanting has faded away, an invisible rhythm, low and sustained, seems to rise upwards. It rolls surely into the hills, exulting in the day just past, and the festivities stretch late into the summer night.

Outside the walls of the arena, native craft vendors display their wares. The powwow is held in August. Information is available from Kamloopa Indian Days Powwow, 345 Yellowhead Highway, Kamloops, BC V2H 1H1, (604) 828-9777.

ART GALLERY, MUSEUM AND ARCHIVES: KAMLOOPS

Overshadowed somewhat by the totem-makers of the Pacific coast, the interior First Nations also display a lively artisitic identity. The Kamloops Art Gallery recently added an important piece of Shuswap art to its permanent collection, a sculpture titled *The Spirit Who Brings the Salmon.* Created in 1993 by Shuswap Ed Archie Noisecat, the sculpture is rendered in alder, maple, copper, abalone, and horsehair. This work is a contemporary expression, but its form is linked to the past aesthetics of the people. Well-recognized ancient Shuswap arts include numerous types of decorated baskets and carved hair combs. Artifacts of sculpted antler knife handles and steatite tobacco pipes with animal faces have been found. At burial sites, sculpted rattlesnakes and human replicas were placed in some graves.

This art gallery periodically sponsors workshops led by native instructors. Past subjects have included native elders hosting instructional sessions on pine needles or birch bark, cedar baskets or how to make traditional copper beads, an artform unique to central interior native people.

The museum, in the same building as the art gallery, displays a permanent collection of artifacts. Before contact, the people of the Shuswap used the Thompson and Fraser rivers as avenues of trade. To

Though this work is officially named *The Spirit Who Brings the Salmon,* it is frequently referred to as the "Noisecat Mask" after its creator.

the coast they transported steatite, jade, dried berries, tanned leathers, red clay paint powder, and mountain goat wool. In return, they received dentalium seashell money, dugout canoes, and oolichan butter. When the fur traders arrived about the 1850s, they utilized the natives' knowledge of waterway routes, which in turn allowed the natives to acquire currency.

The art gallery keeps a list of native Shuswap artists who are available to create custom artworks. Information is available from the Kamloops Art Gallery, 207 Seymour Street, Kamloops, BC V2C 2E7, (604) 828-3543, fax (604) 828-0662. Information is also available from the Kamloops Museum and Archives, 207 Seymour Street, Kamloops, BC V2C 2E7, (604) 828-3576.

Sockeye Run: The Adams River

Nearly 500 km inland from the Pacific Ocean, a small tributary of the Thompson River only 11 km long is the spawning ground for one of North America's largest sockeye runs. In October 1989, only 79 fish arrived; in October 1990—over 2 million. The Adams River sockeye run has always shown strong four-year cycles; occasionally, two consecutive dominant runs will occur. Scientists are not quite sure why—but historical records back to 1793 suggest this has always been so. Dominant runs of more than two million sockeye are expected in 1994 and 1998. The spectacle is a moving one.

Unlike most other salmon species, sockeye spend their first year in lakes. After a year, they migrate downstream to the ocean, where they feed and grow for about 2 years before returning to spawn. The Fraser River, with several stillwater lakes along its length such as Kamloops and Shuswap lakes, is ideal for these fish, which must swim an incredible distance inland to reach their spawning ground.

The natives were kind to the salmon. However, loggers and railway builders were less concerned. In 1913, an enormous landslide caused by faulty railroad construction blocked a dominant run. Disastrous as that was, the run was already suffering from the blockages caused by a logging slash dam built earlier. Finally,

Dominant runs in the Adams River occur every four years. The journey of the salmon—the ebbing and flowing of their cycle—is all part of the mystery of the river.

in 1945, to halt the accelerating decline in fish, the government built a concrete fishway at Hells Gate. By 1958, the dominant run was up to 15 million. Today, in a single day, commercial fishing operations on the lower Fraser River can capture more than 1 million returning fish. From 6 to 11 million fish are caught en route.

Every year, biologists monitor the run. By measuring the plankton levels in the lakes and investigating the lake trout that gorge on sockeye eggs, they can monitor the conditions that disturb the fry. Significantly, the entire length of the Adams River, from Adams Lake to Shuswap Lake, is now protected in Roderick Haig-Brown Provincial Park. If the sockeye make it upstream, past the commercial fish boats and native fishers, they can spawn in peace.

Roderick Haig-Brown Provincial Park and Conservation Area, north off the highway between Kamloops and Salmon Arm, also contains extensive evidence of early First Nations habitation. Kekuli pithouse depressions and pictographs can be seen. Information is available from the Thompson River District, BC Parks, 1265 Dalhousie Drive, Kamloops, BC V2C 5Z5, (604) 828-4494.

QUAAOUT LODGE: CHASE

The Quaaout Lodge is owned by the Little Shuswap Band. Constructed in the shape of a traditional kekuli pithouse, the rooms are spacious and the cuisine is excellent.

One ancient Okanagan and Shuswap story tells of the first meeting between natives and whites in the region. The story makes it evident that the native tradition here is one of hospitality. Following is an excerpt from the story.

Pela-ka-mu-lah-uh spent a great deal of time travelling. On one buffalo hunt to the area now known as Montana, he met the first white men he had ever seen. He thought they were beautiful, not human beings, but spirits come to do good for his people. He escorted two of them west to his home over the mountains. When he had

to leave again, a ceremony was held and he asked his chief to take care of them. Upon that occasion, Pela-ka-mu-lah-uh made a famous speech.

"From my waters, I drink, you drink. From my fruits, I eat, you eat. From my game, I eat, you eat..... I have plenty of everything, enough for all of us...."

The hospitality evident in this story can still be felt today at the native-owned Quaaout Lodge. Opened in 1992 and built at a cost of $4.3 million, the resort was the culmination of ten years of planning by the Little Shuswap Indian Band.

The resort incorporates several aboriginal styles into its design. Held aloft by a dozen 12-metre lodgepole

pine rafters, the circular lobby echoes a traditional kekuli pithouse. The black slate floor is etched with large reproductions of pictographs found at nearby Copper Island. The central hammered-copper fireplace blazes away on chilly evenings. Each of the 71 rooms has a view of the lake, and there are six special king-size units, each with their own hot tubs and fireplaces. All rooms are well-appointed with upholstery and curtains in an Indian design. General amenities include a swimming pool, hot tub, sauna, and outdoor exercise area. Meeting planners can take advantage of two meeting rooms and courteous catering services. The restaurant and its outside patios can accommodate 150 people. Special barbeques can be arranged for parties of five or more.

The Quaaout Lodge is situated on a large beachfront property and there are several interesting activities nearby. One special touch appeals to youngsters. In front of the resort are five teepees for rent at a nominal rate. Nearby Roderick Haig-Brown Provincial Park is famous for its sockeye run, with dominant runs every four years; 1994, 1998, 2002, etc. Pithouse replicas are located at nearby parks. There are miles of developed trails; all guests are requested to borrow a bear-bell from the front desk before walking in the woods. Sailboats and canoes are available for boating to nearby Copper Island, famous for cliffside pictographs and numerous deer.

Several archaeological excavations have been carried out in the area. Besides the depressions of pithouse villages, researchers have uncovered the remains of underground baking ovens, food caches, plant-gathering sites, and "deer funnels"—laneways which were used to assist in the hunt.

To arrive via the Trans-Canada Highway, turn north at the Squilax Bridge turnoff, 7 km east of Chase. Information is available from the Quaaout Lodge, Box 1215, Chase, BC V0E 1M0, (604) 679-3090, 1-800-663-4303, fax (604) 679-3039. The Skwlax Powwow, held in July at Chase, is open to the public. For information, phone (604) 679-3090.

Beside the lodge, basic teepees are available for rent at a nominal fee. No bedding is provided.

Famed for Their Hospitality

Now in her second year of employment at Quaaout Lodge, Julie John enjoys her job. "It's only natural my people built the lodge," John says. "Native people have always been famous for their hospitality." Unfortunately, the hospitality business occupies much of her time. She has no time to dance at the local powwows anymore.

"The best thing is meeting all the people who pass through. As well as Canadians, we have had guests from Germany, England, New Zealand, California — yes, lots of Americans. I enjoy talking with them all."

TRADITIONAL NATIVE CUISINE: MODERN STYLE

In Vancouver, the Quilicum Restaurant has a well-honed menu of traditional favourites. From time to time, Isadora's Restaurant on Granville Island offers a native-inspired menu. Pictured above is a meal prepared at the Quaaout Lodge.

With the abundant food sources available to them, indigenous people of the coast and the interior developed their own forms of cooking. However, it is only in recent years that their food and style of cooking has begun to come to the attention of the culinary world.

In 1992, Andrew George, a Coast Salish from North Vancouver, was part of a Canadian native team that travelled to the World Culinary Olympics in Frankfurt, Germany. There, his team won two gold medals. "Adapting traditional foods to contemporary tastes is not my greatest problem," George says, "it is getting financing to open a restaurant specializing in native foods," At the time of writing, George was in the process of setting up a restaurant in Smithers, B.C.

At present, it is possible to taste formal B.C. native cuisine at two native-owned resorts. The Tsa.Kwa.Luten Lodge on Vancouver Island serves native-style foods in a soaring Great Room. The Quaaout Lodge at Chase has an innovative menu planned by the chiefs, elders, and native women of the Little Shuswap band. Their intent is to include enough wild meat on the menu to permit other tribal members to set up venison and waterfowl farms.

In Vancouver, the Quilicum Restaurant has a well-honed menu of traditional favourites. From time to time, Isadora's Restaurant on Granville Island offers a native-inspired menu.

October is called wul-êt'-sun-uh meaning "not yet time for salmon"
—Kwakwaka'wakw'

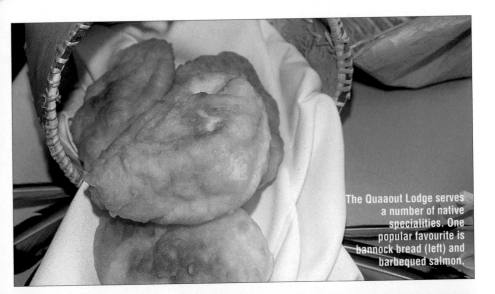

The Quaaout Lodge serves a number of native specialities. One popular favourite is bannock bread (left) and barbequed salmon.

Native Foods Adapted to Modern Tastes

Herring roe on kelp
Bannock breads
Smoked salmon
Indian candy dried salmon
Steamed clams
Marinated caribou
Steamed prawns
Barbequed oysters
Pan-fried oolichans
Whipped soopolallie ice cream
Sweet potato with hazel nuts
Clam fritters
Salmon on bannock
Barbequed halibut
Seaweed and rice
Chilled raspberry soup
Salmonberry sweet cakes
Roast venison
Steamed dulse (seaweed)
Tla-o-quiaht chinook salmon
Barbequed rabbit
Crab in the shell
Smoked black Alaska cod
Barbequed duck
Dried seaweed snacks
Moose stew
Sta'mish salad with wind-dried
  salmon

Furniture Maker and Carver

"We are out to create a whole lot of unique furniture," says **Wayne Eustache,** "from boardroom tables to bed headboards." Presently working on an 18-metre totem pole, Eustache and his team also turn out masks, bowls, and traditional serving dishes. Yellow cedar and red cedar are his favourite media. Born in Kamloops to Interior Salish parents, Eustache later moved to Vancouver. "When I'm into my carving, I never worry," Wayne says.

He adds that his style is an amalgamation of interior and coastal influences.

Information on Eustache and his company, First Nations Furniture and Art Co., is available from Tradeworks, Suite 210, 830 East 7th Ave, Vancouver, (604) 873-3775.

JOURNEY TO THE LAND OF THE MOUNTAIN GODS: TRADE ROUTE

Siskiutl, a two-headed sea monster who was friendly to mariners, is depicted in blue colours that pick up the hues of the sun-bleached sky. The Bella Coola native school is constructed of cedar wood, reflecting the deep forest's natural tones.

From Williams Lake to the ocean at Bella Coola, Highway 20 — sometimes called the "Great Freedom Highway" — offers several native awareness adventures for modern-day explorers. While there is not a stop sign for 456 km, the pavement does stop — at Nimpo Lake. After that, the wide gravel road is well maintained. Passing through spectacular scenery and ranching and native communities, the road heads into Tweedsmuir Provincial Park. There, motorists encounter the dangerous Heckman Pass (see box). Arriving on the valley floor, Norwegian-influenced Hägensborg is located near native-occupied Bella Coola.

From east to west there are several stops of interest:
- The Cariboo Friendship Society welcomes visitors. The society and its Hearth Restaurant are located at 99 South Third Avenue, Williams Lake, (604) 398-6831, fax (604) 398-6115. There are a few Interior Salish artifacts at the Williams Lake Museum, 1148 Broadway, (604) 392-4360.
- Farwell Canyon and a bighorn sheep range are located together. Native fishing families from the Chilcotin Band camp along

"Chilcotin" means people of the blue water.

the river. The area is home to more than one-fifth of the world population of California Bighorn Sheep.
- A plaque commemorates the 1884 Chilcotin War. Believing they had intentionally been given blankets contaminated with smallpox, a band of Chilcotin warriors ambushed a camp of road surveyors. To the Chilcotins, it was a righteous war to end conquest. To the whites, it was murder. Led by their warchief Klatassine, the ambushers fled homeward. They were soon

pursued by two mounted field expeditions. The plaque is located 5 km west of Nimpo Lake, just off Highway 20.

- The Rainbow Range is located at the eastern entrance to Tweedsmuir Provincial Park. The range is volcanic in origin and was a prime source of obsidian, a volcanic glass used to make sharp tools and knives. Information is available from BC Parks, Cariboo District, 540 Borland St, Williams Lake, BC V2R 1R8, (604) 398-4414, fax (604) 398-4686.
- Stuie, in the Atnarko River valley, was a native trading camp long before white contact. Traders would meet here to assemble their goods and pack their loads. At the site are unexcavated smoke houses, petroglyphs, and a burial site. The site is unmarked. Information is available in person from the park headquarters about 10 km east of Stuie.
- The Nuxälk-Carrier natives first blazed the trails later used by Sir Alexander Mackenzie's expedition. MacKenzie made the first land crossing of the continent in 1793. He completed his epic journey more than twelve years before the famed Lewis and Clark expedition across the western United States.
- The Bella Coola Band will allow accompanied visitors to visit their petroglyphs. The Acswalcta School features excellent examples of west coast native art.

For information on Highway 20, contact the Travel InfoCentre, 1148 Broadway South, Highway 97 South, Williams Lake, BC V2G 1A2, (604) 392-5025, fax (604) 392-4214. Travel information is also available from the Bella Coola Seasonal InfoCentre, Box 670, Bella Coola, V0T 1C0, (604) 799-5919. The Chief Anahim Annual Powwow is held in Anahim in May, (604) 394-4293.

Difficult Road: Heckman Pass

At the east side of Tweedsmuir Provincial Park, motorists encounter Heckman Pass, also known as "The Hill." Provincial authorities considered the pass unsuitable for a proper road, so in 1953, the locals equipped themselves with a bulldozer and built the road themselves. The result is a washboard gravel road with a formidible grade of 18 percent. Over a distance of 25 km, the road drops 1524 metres to sea level. While the switchbacks provide breathtaking views of the mountains, the road may be impassable for heavy campervans. Check all vehicle brakes before setting out. There are two roadside pullout areas on The Hill, please use them.

The Cariboo Highways Department, (604) 398-4510, fax (604) 398-4454, will give updates on the condition of the road.

NATIVE TRADITIONAL FISHING: FARWELL CANYON

In 1993, Walt Disney Productions shot a scene at this remote location. They edited out the native fish camps, but feature a helicopter chase between the "bad guys" and FBI agents, an improbable occurrence for this area.

Before the arrival of white settlers, the Chilcotin people lived in small groups on a scenic plateau. They fished in season, and gathered fruits, herbs, and wild potatoes. Experts at processing hides, they also hunted and trapped. The Chilcotin natives who live here today carry on in much the same way.

During late July and August, local natives catch salmon from the banks of the Chilcotin River. The river cuts through sandstone cliffs. Poised on the rocks, young men use longhandled dipnets to snare returning salmon. The fish are taken to a nearby camp, prepared, and placed on hanging racks to dry. A slow-burning fire in a small temporary hut finishes the process. Families camp out beside the river. Each family prepares fish for several other families. Nearby, a pictograph attests to the long-time importance of this fishing spot.

Trade was an important activity between all the tribes that lived in the area. The Chilcotin who live on this plateau; the Bella Coola, who live among the tall coastal mountains; and the Shuswap, who live throughout the Cariboo, traded with each other. In turn, the Shuswap made their way to trade with the people of the prairies.

Along the coast, a small smelt-fish, the oolichan, was also an important trade good. A dried oolichan is so oily it can be burned as a candle. Schools of oolichan return in two- to four-year cycles. In season, millions were netted. The Bella Coola natives netted many, but word of a dominant run would spread quickly. Other bands would travel to the coast and buy temporary rights to capture their own supply. The fish were placed in pits and weighted down to process out the oily fat. This tasty fat was scooped off and placed in wooden boxes. It could be stored for about two years. Interior tribes, other coastal groups, and bands from as far away as the prairies, prized the tasty spread. It was normal to dip dried berries and salmon pieces into the fat to add flavour, much as we use butter.

The Chilcotin fishing area is occupied in season, usually July and August; phone to confirm that the salmon have arrived. Do not interfere with the fishers or the drying racks. Visitors may watch from the bridge. If walking down to the camp, please bring generous gifts of food. Ask permission from adults before

Harriet Tenale, a Tootie Chilcotin woman, helps to prepare dried salmon for several families. "The bears stole about 40 pounds of processed salmon one night," she shyly admits. "They make lots more work for us."

Special Adventures: Departures from the Cariboo

Native Wilderness Adventures, RR 3, Box 10, Sugar Cane, Williams Lake, BC V2G 1M3; five days at a native camp, traditional foods, sweat lodge, native crafts, teepee accommodation.

Cariboo Tourist Association, 190 Yorkston Ave, Box 4900, Williams Lake, BC V2G 2V8, (604)392-2226, 1-800-663-5885, fax (604) 392-2838; a list of native hunting guides, trail rides, guest ranches, and mountain climbing guides.

photographing individuals, including children. This is a traditional area and natives have the right to carry on without acknowledging visitors or being disturbed.

To reach the fish camps from Highway 20, travel 49 km west of Williams Lake, turn south at the Farwell Canyon turnoff, continue for 20 km to the bridge. Young men fish under the bridge in season. The pictographs are found across the bridge up a footpath. The drying camps are located beside the river; cross the bridge, then walk down to the river. Watch for bears.

Information is available from the Travel InfoCentre, 1148 Broadway South, Highway 97 South, Williams Lake, BC V2G 1A2, (604) 392-5025, fax (604) 392-4214.

Petroglyph Site: Bella Coola

Ancient figures silently call out messages whose words are forever inaudible. But human hearts still struggle to hear what they say. There are stories among the Bella Coola natives that many eons ago, Polynesian people came to visit them. For a long time, they feasted together and rejoiced at their accomplishments. To immortalize the feat of crossing the ocean, they chipped out a number of petroglyph figures that can be seen today.

Anthropologists have no way of confirming these storie, but will attest to the spectacular and ancient nature of this site. Hundreds of petroglyphs have fallen from a cliff-face and are knotted among tall tree roots in a deep forest. Some of the faces are Polynesian in likeness, while others bespeak more recent origins. The exact meaning of all petroglyphs is lost in time.

The petroglyph site may be viewed in the company of a native guide, who requires a fee. Do not disturb the site; removal of any artifact is punishable by law. Small reproductions of the petroglyphs are available in stone from Portfolio West, 1092 Hamilton Street, Vancouver, BC V6B 2R9, (604) 685-6554. Information on hiring a guide is available from the Bella Coola Band Office, (604) 799-5613; or from Bella Coola's Goodwill Ambassador, Darren Edgar, Box 549, Bella Coola, BC V0T 1C0, (604) 799-5449

Like a river of light, sunbeams were seen as a pathway to Earth for spiritual entities. Called a "sky journey," visitors from other realms found their way to Earth aboard these strands of piercing light.

NUXÄLK-CARRIER GREASE TRAIL: QUESNEL TO BELLA COOLA

T he Nuxälk-Carrier, or Alexander Mackenzie Heritage Trail is a foot-trail some 250 km long running from the mouth of the Blackwater River (West Road) to Dean Channel on th ewest coast. The route follows native "grease" trails that were traversed in 1793 by Alexander Mackenzie. He was the first European to make a successful overland crossing of the continent. The explorer and his party took fourteen days to cross the plateau and arrive in Bella Coola.

Though Alexander Mackenzie and his 25 men spent much of their journey paddling on rivers in an 8-metre canoe, when they reached Quesnel, they made the trek overland. The native people of the area, the Nuxälk and Sekani-Carrier, had mixed reactions to the strange group. Some were hospitable, others beat drums and threatened them, still others fled their homes, leaving their campfires smouldering. What is notable is that Mackenzie's diary records that he encountered native bands, "every few hours." Tragically, after introduced diseases had devastated the bands, travellers along the same route in the 1930s went for days without meeting a native person. Today, the native population throughout British Columbia is increasing.

Though he was the first European through their territory, Mackenzie noted their use of iron utensils and foreign

Natives used dogs for packing and hunting.

tools. The path his party traversed was known as a "grease trail," after oolichan grease, a prized trade good in the area.

Today, 14 days is the amount of time recommended by the Alexander Mackenzie Trail Association for expert hikers to cover the route; intermediate hikers should allow 24 days. It may be necessary to arrange a food drop. The modern trail follows Mackenzie's diary description of the route. It is a challenging path. While the full length of the trail may only be attempted by serious

backpacking hikers, there are several shorter walks from trailhead points along High-way 20. Escorted tours by horseback, snowmobile, cross-country ski or air are also popular. Information is available from the Alexander Mackenzie Trail Association, Box 425, Station A, Kelowna, BC V1Y 7P1, (604) 992-8716, 1-800-663-5885, fax (604) 992-9606. A detailed fold-out trail guidebook is available for C$20.00.

> *We who had not advantage of the Indian's education and experience, were often in imminent danger.*
> —Alexander Mackenzie, 1792

PURCHASE YOUR OWN TEEPEE: CRESTON

Ktunaxa native Wilfred Jacob and his family have been manufacturing tepees commercially since 1991. "Before that, some of our bands had to rent them from whites," Jacob says. Today, their customers range from movie production teams to native and non-native customers from as far away as Germany. "We even provide whole teepee villages."

True teepees are not symmetrical cones, but a tilted cone, that is steeper at the back. "The technology is more intricate than people think. People should know where to pitch their teepees, too," says Jacob. Long ago buffalo-hide teepees covered the plains. In this region, teepees were covered with tule, a bulrush (or sedge) type of plant often used for making mats. Canvas is now the material of choice. A properly made teepee is well-lit, well-ventilated, and cool in summer. When properly oriented, it is sturdy against high winds and heavy rains.

Combining the technical skills of modern tentmaking with centuries of Ktunaxa know-how, the Jacob family will customize a teepee "while you wait." In about three hours, customers can walk away with a lap-seamed teepee canvas, ready to pitch. Popular models range in diameter from 3 to 7 m. A modern teepee costs between $300 to $1000, depending upon its size. New teepees are unpainted, leaving room for personal creativity.

The Jacob family invites visitors to view their manufacturing operation. It is located in a 23-m teepee on the side of the highway. In summer, they also manufacture bark-covered canoes. Information is available from the Ktunaxa Tipi Company, Box 5, Site 7, RR1, Creston, BC V0B 1G0, (604) 428-4582.

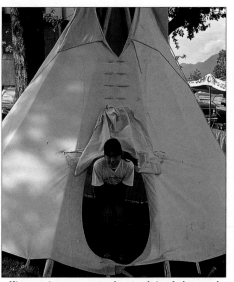

Ktunaxa teepees come in a variety of sizes and can be custom-made in about three hours.

How To Paint Your Own Teepee

- Create designs that are meaningful to you. Do not copy teepee patterns from books. No two teepees are ever painted alike. Ideally, the design should come to you in a dream or a vision.
- Designs at the base of a teepee represent the earth, the door level represents the life of humans, and the top refers to the sky and spirit world. One area may dominate the others on your teepee.
- Designs have meaning, primarily to the teepee owner. Hoops may represent unity, zig zigs may be lightning storms, animals stand for their attributes. More stripes mean bigger medicine.
- Colours are symbolic, but not the same to all nations. Blue, red, and yellow bands together may mean sacred objects inside. Black may be night, blue may be north; red, the morning sun; and yellow, the evening sun.
- Teepees should not be painted on the inside, though an inner teepee liner may be painted with decorative strips and stories of conquest.
- Use ordinary housepaint.

LUSSIER UNDEVELOPED HOTSPRINGS: KIMBERLEY AREA

Experiencing the cold of the nearby river contrasted with the warmth of the natural hot springs, makes the drive along a narrow gravel road worthwhile.

Native people believed in the efficacy of spa waters. In several places, they declared the area around a hot springs to be sacred and, like a modern demilitarized zone, warring enemies could enter the area without danger. After a battle, enemies would often sit together and soothe their wounds in the warm waters.

There were said to be whispering spirits that inhabit the regions around a hot spring. It is possible to hear the spirits but is impossible to make out what they are saying. Any native person who discovered a new hot springs was greatly honoured, and the band considered them to be favoured by the spirits.

In the Kootenays, there are several such areas. Fairmont Hot Springs and Radium Hot Springs are now commercial resorts complete with swimming pool complexes, hotels, and golf courses. Ainsworth Hot Springs is modestly developed.

Lussier is a hot springs site that remains in its original state. To make the stream warmer, visitors move a stone and divert the hot water. To cool off, they move it again to allow cold stream water to enter. In wintertime, the warm waters attract reptiles; in summer, this is not a problem.

Lussier is near Kimberley, Wasa, and Skookumchuck. Travel toward Whiteswan Provincial Park and Top-of-the-World Provincial Park along a narrow mountain gravel road for 17 km. The site is marked by a small unserviced change room at the side of the road. There are many steps down to the river. Information is available from the Kimberley Travel InfoCentre, 350 Ross Street, Kimberley, BC V1A 2Z9, (604) 427-3666, fax (604) 427-5378.

> *Ease pain by your great magic, so that I may feel well.*
> — Many tribal groups, invocation for health

NATIVE ART GALLERY: PRINCE GEORGE

ABOVE: A grove of paper white birches is sometimes filled with the rat-tat-tat of woodpeckers. **INSERT:** Birchbark-biting art (here, adorned with dentalia shells) visually embodies that experience as an artform.

The natives on far away Vancouver Island prospered by collecting rare dentalia shells that were used as money by natives across North America. In many tribes, daughters who wore a dentalia necklace could expect to marry well. Among the Yuquot of California, one necklace-length string bought a slave, three strings bought a house, and for the crime of murder, the fine was fifteen strings. White traders quickly discovered their value and even commissioned a company in England to make counterfeit copies out of porcelain. An 1801 ship manifest reports 40,000 dentalia shells in the hold. The natives were not fooled.

Phil Nuytten runs a Vancouver undersea diving company and is dedicated to researching the shells. "As they (the shells) got farther from their source, the stories got more fanciful," he says. Here in Carrier country, it was said they anchored a human corpse in deep water to attract dentalium creatures. Nuytten says this is untrue. On Vancouver Island, he discovered a mop-like contraption mounted on a long pole. It was used to collect the deep water shells at the rate of about twenty per day.

Birchbark-biting art is another of the interesting art forms found at this gallery. Once practised by woodland women here and across the prairies, today it has been revived by native Angelique Levac, Prince George, and other native women in Saskatchewan. Originally used as a method of recalling a quillwork design, the works are produced by folding the bark and carefully biting in a pattern. No two designs are alike.

Information is available from the Prince George Native Art Gallery, 144 George St, Prince George, BC V2L 1P9, (604) 562-7385; or Angelique Levac, RR 2, Site 1 Comp 144, Prince George, BC V2N 2H9, (604) 962-5463. The Lheit-Lit 'En Nation Heritage Society Annual Powwow is held in August, (604) 963-8451.

TRADITIONAL NATIVE FISHING: KYAH WIGET

ABOVE: Where the river suddenly narrows and plunges into a canyon, young native fishers stand on the rocks and gaff salmon. **INSERT:** Dressed for show, a native fisher with gaff illustrates how he would have appeared some time ago.

rom strategic places on rock outcroppings along the canyon walls, Carrier Wet'suwet'en natives gaff salmon with long poles. TheBulkley River suddenly narrows from about 700 m to an opening only 15 m wide. As the river seethes and boils, then plunges into the canyon, salmon are sometimes hurled into the air. Waiting for them on the steep canyon walls, the natives stand poised, spears at the ready. The natives call this place *Kyah Wiget* meaning "old village." On shore nearby, native women prepare the fish and hang it on racks to dry

Outsiders may observe native fishing activities as they occur today. The camp is occupied in season, usually July and August; phone to confirm that the salmon have arrived. If spending time among the people, a gift of food is appropriate. Do not disturb the natives at work; ask permission of the adults before photographing individuals, including children. This is a traditional area and natives have the right to carry on without acknowledging visitors or being disturbed.

Kyah Wiget, more commonly known as Moricetown Canyon, is located on the side of Highway 16, 37 km west of Smithers. Information is available from the Smithers InfoCentre, Box 2379, 1425 Main Street, Smithers, BC V0J 2N0, (604) 847-9854, fax (604) 847-3337.

Native Salmon Camp Day Tour: Prince George

From July through September, visitors may arrange to take a jetboat ride on the Fraser River. Arriving at the traditional site of the Lheit-Lit'en Nations Elder's Salmon Fishing Camp, native tour leaders point out traditional methods of harvesting and preparing salmon. The photograph shows the old method of splitting a salmon for drying, head and all. A feast of traditional native food follows. Allow four hours. There are two departures each day. Information is available from the Lheit-Lit'en Nations Elders Salmon Camp Tour, Fort George Canyon, RR 1, Site 27, Comp 60, Prince George, BC V2N 2H8, (604) 963-8451, fax (604) 963-8324.

PEOPLE OF THE MOUNTAINS

Storm clouds born of the great plains gather in the mountains. Western-based tribes found the buffalo and furs good incentives to cross the challenging barrier. But harsh weather, disease, and the Blackfoot Confederacy discouraged them from settling permanently on the eastern side of the Rockies.

In ancient times, only a few people lived full-time in the area now known as the "Rockies." Both to the east and to the west, food was more abundant. Bison roamed the eastern prairies; fishing and hunting were good in the western forests. However, it seems that the mountains were well-visited. As evidenced by arrowheads, flint-sharpeners, and animal bone remains, parties of prehistoric hunters entered the mountains over a period of thousands of years. In 1969, an archaeological team identified 122 butchering sites throughout the four mountain national parks area.

During the 1600s, the mountains saw more activity. At various times, the Stoney, Cree, Ktunaxa, and Beaver people all left their marks in these mountains. Long before the first whites arrived, some came to live, then withdrew because of the harsh conditions. Others came and prospered in the fur trading business, until they were wiped out by smallpox. Still others came and remain today.

Spirit People

The interior people honoured animals in a somewhat different way from the people on the prairie or the people on the coast.

On the coast, clan members saw themselves as related to animals and spiritual beings by birth. On the prairies, the buffalo and the White Buffalo were important spirits that could be called up by medicine men. The interior people saw animals as figures related to the span of a human life.

Coyote	Trickster	Youth
Bear	Caring Parent	Parenthood
Owl	Wise Person	Maturity
Eagle	Spiritual Being	Ageless

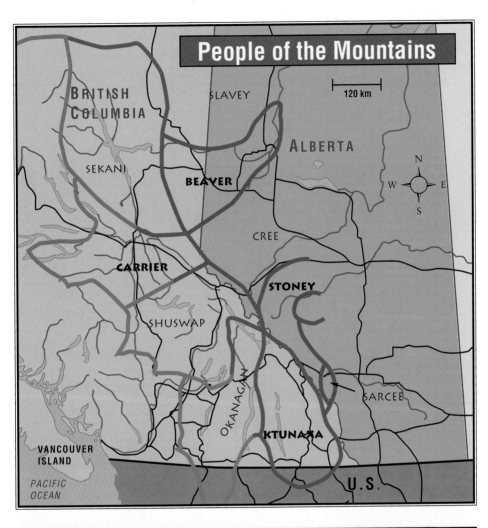

People of the Mountains

BRITISH COLUMBIA

SLAVEY

120 km

ALBERTA

SEKANI

BEAVER

CREE

CARRIER

STONEY

SHUSWAP

N
W · E
S

SARCEE

OKANAGAN

KTUNAXA

VANCOUVER
ISLAND

PACIFIC
OCEAN

U.S.

Sunfeather Woman

Flora Mark is manager of the Chiniki Handicraft Centre in Morley. Born to Stoney parents, she keeps busy running the store and raising two sons who are half Cree. Though it is somewhat less exciting than nearby, tourist-filled Banff, she prefers that her boys grow up on the reserve. Mark carefully stocks the store with interesting local items, all native-made in western Canada. "We keep expanding our selection of jewellery, art, and clothing," she says. Her personal favourite is the Sunfeather clothing line. Information is available from the Chiniki Restaurant and Handicraft Centre, Morley, AB T0L 1N0, (403) 881-3960

The Stoney or Nakoda people, who today live in the Morley area, are descendants of the people who survived. Long ago related to the Sioux, who in turn are related to the Assiniboine, their name derives from their old-time cooking practises of dropping hot stones into vessels to boil water. They prefer to call themselves the Nakoda "the people," as distinguished from their Dakota cousins to the south.

They are noted for the alliances they formed with the Cree, ever to be on guard against the warring Blackfoot.

Today, members of the Cree nations live mostly in east-central Alberta. But in the 1800s, white fur traders and the Cree, more or less in tandem, moved west as far as the Rockies. The Cree darted about in pursuit of buffalo and fur-bearing animals, keeping a wary eye out for enemies. Devoting much of their time to trapping for the white traders, alcoholism and disease were the heavy toll of that close

relationship.

With the soft tread of their moccasins forever gone from the modern-day Rockies, there are two other tribes whose story is interwoven into these peaks: the Ktunaxa and the Beaver. For a time, their well-developed routes criss-crossed the Rockies. The fur trade brought a period of prosperity, then unrest—soon followed by soul-crushing plagues.

The Ktunaxa people probably knew the mountain passes best. They regularly crossed from their western headquarters to hunt buffalo. Returning home in the winter, they sought to avoid the ever-vigilant Blackfoot Confederacy. Eventually, a few settled permanently in the eastern foothills. But in the mid-1700s, and periodically thereafter, smallpox decimated their numbers to extinction. Today Ktunaxa people are found only on the western side.

The Beaver are Déné people whose traditions arose from living along the upper waters of the Peace River in

the north. Excellent moose hunters and trappers, they were also confident hunting guides.

Some left their homes to try their luck in the Rockies. Using the acquisition of the gun to good advantage, the Beaver cooperated with whites during the time of the fur trade. Along with the Cree, they displaced the Sekani nation. Like many bands, they suffered greatly from introduced diseases. By 1900, there were only 46 Beaver people available to sign Treaty No. Eight. Always praised by whites for their modest ways, it did little to protect them. In 1913, most of them were suffering from tuberculosis. Families had scattered; a few returned north to their homeland, only to find it carved up into small reserves.

A Story About Mountain Hot Springs

The hot springs in and around Banff were well known to the Stoney, Blackfoot, Blood, Sarcee, and Peigan people. It is said that warring enemies would sometimes sit together in the pools to heal their wounds. Upon receiving any healing benefits, they would leave an offering of thanks. But since the white people have come, no prayers are said and no thanks are given. It is said the waters are losing their powers.

INDIAN PONIES AND HORSES

Mr. and Mrs. John Hunter, Stoney natives

There appear to have been wild horses native to North America. However, these herds died out in prehistoric times. It took the exploits of the Spanish conquistadores in Central America in the 1500s to re-introduce the animal to this continent. The horses they left behind changed the face of aboriginal life particularly across the plains of North America.

Early in the 1600s, and long before the arrival of whites, the animals that the Peigan nation first described as "big elk-dogs" quickly became a sought-after commodity. By the late 1700s, horses were relatively common in most areas east of the Rockies.

Native cultures adapted rapidly to their introduction and the people were skilled riders. Horses were used as beasts of burden, they evened-up the odds in hunting buffalo, they gave a warrior a great advantage over an unmounted enemy, and they naturally became a symbol of wealth.

A whole ethic evolved around "acquiring" horses. By trade or by raid, horses were in great demand. Tribes that were adept at acquiring horses soon displaced those who were not.

Ceremonial periods were set aside to add to horse stocks. First, spirit songs were devised to protect their own mounts. Then, the bravest men were selected for raids. Benefits flowed to those bands and individuals who met with success.

When Christian missionaries arrived, there were great misunderstandings on both sides. The missionaries fretted that the natives had no concept of "sin." In turn, the natives thought the missionaries were quite insane to suggest they could burn in hell simply for acquiring animals that brought their people such great benefits.

> *If I have good luck and get home safely, please allow me to be the victim at the Sun Dance.*
> —A Blood elder, 1947, recounting the youthful prayer he recited when stealing horses

Mountain Passes and Stolen Horses

The area now known as Kananaskis Country has always been a popular mountain pass. In early spring, prairie people traversed its valleys to acquire horses. During the summer, transient western tribes re-acquired them. Some horses were so familiar with the routine that they escaped by themselves. Crossing the mountains alone, the animals turned up east of the Rockies in the spring and on the western side in the autumn. To stop this from occurring, stolen horses were either tied to an old mare, or their noses were rubbed with animal musk gland scents to confuse their homing instincts.

PAINT POTS: KOOTENAY NATIONAL PARK

ABOVE: Red powders, such as those mined here, are found in sacred amulets and in the stones around sacred sites. INSET: An active medicine woman's pouches display red ochre powders and other precious pigments of cinnabar, sand, and ebony black.

In earlier times, native tribes from both the prairies and the mountains travelled to a place in the Kootenay River valley to obtain "red earth." A vast hill of iron oxide—a bright rust colour—is found around the outlets of three cold mineral springs. Though ochre is technically a yellow artist's pigment, the material here is frequently referred to as red ochre. Over geologic time, cones of red iron deposits had built up around each pool, first providing natives with the basic ingredient in paint. The red powder was cleaned, kneaded with water, formed into walnut-sized balls, and flattened into cakes. The cakes were baked in a fire, then ground into powder. The powder was used as war-paint, but also for pianting teepees, clothes, and pictographs. They experimented with the material for medicine and used it in ceremonials. Experts find evidence that aboriginal people all over the world associated red paint powder with blood, therefore, with life itself.

In the view of the Stoney people, a big animal spirit and a thunder spirit reside at this hot spring. While they report sometimes hearing something like a flute calling them to war, they could never make out the messages clearly nor could they make out the exact shapes of the spirits. The word "medicine" in plains culture is synonymous with the word "mystery."

Kootenay National Park Paint Pots are located along Highway 93 in Vermillion Pass, north of Radium Hot Springs. Highway signs point out the site. The roadside walk is .5 km to the pools.

Information is available from Canadian Parks Service, Box 220, Radium Hot Springs, BC V0A 1M0, (604) 347-9615, fax (604) 347-9980.

Usna'waki-cabugi' means "where the red clay spirit is taken."
—Stoney, expression

TAKAKKAW FALLS: YOHO NATIONAL PARK

This 380-metre high waterfall is fed from the meltwaters of the unseen Daly Glacier located immediately behind the cascade. The glacier is backed by the Waputik Icefield. In summer during warm weather, the plunging mountain torrent roars with a heavy volume of water. In autumn, the melt slows; and by winter, the raging waterfall has narrowed to a trickle of ice.

Though *takakkaw* means "it is magnificent" in Cree, the natives were not fond of the spirits at this place. They referred to it as a place of evil. Because of the fluctuations in flow, the waterfall can be moody and the wet rock cliffs can present a dark ominous face.

Takakkaw Falls is located in Yoho National Park near Field on Highway 1. Highway signs point out a narrow paved road to the falls; there are sharp switchbacks.

This valley is now known to contain ancient fossils of great rarity. Researchers from around the world come here to unearth and study the fossil specimens. The Burgess Shales are protected *in situ* for educational purposes by the UNESCO World Heritage Site program. Periodically, evening programs are presented at an outdoor amphitheatre located in one of the nearby campgrounds. These programs explain the value of the shales and the history of their discov-

In winter, Takakkaw Falls freezes to a solid icy gash. The icy surface is popular with mountaineers.

ery. Some researchers indicate that they are the most important fossils being uncovered in the world today.

Information is available from the Canadian Parks Service, Box 99, Field, BC V0A 1H0, (604) 343-6324.

LAKE OF LITTLE FISHES: LAKE LOUISE

At sunrise, the iridescent rainbow can still be seen shimmering in the waters of Lake Louise.

Now enjoying fame as "Banff's Lake Louise, Jewel of the Canadian Rockies," the native people more humbly called this ice-water—the "lake of little fishes."

Undoubtedly one of the most beautifully coloured lakes in the world, there is an ancient Stoney story about its origins.

Long ago, a tribe of giants lived upon the land. One was a great hunter. But he was never satisfied. One day he saw a rainbow arced across the flat prairie. He decided it would make a fine bow for hunting — for a fine man like him. Following the rainbow, he travelled into the mountains. There he ascended the top of a high peak. Climbing the tallest tree, he tried to reach the sky. But time after time, just as he managed to touch it, it would disappear. During his final attempt, he angrily caught the tip of the rainbow and hurled it against the nearest mountain. Augh! It broke into three pieces. One part shattered completely on the mountain peak; one piece was hurled into the valley; another slid down the snowy mountain and sank into the lake. After many moons deep within the water, some of the colours found each other. They rejoiced and regained their lustre. Slowly they spread, suffusing the lake. Today at sunrise the colours can be seen iridescent in the water. And, after a storm, another third of the broken rainbow can be seen arced over the side of the lake.

Lake of Little Fishes is located 58 km northwest of Banff on Highway 1. Information is available from the Banff Chamber of Commerce, Box 1298, Banff, AB T0L 0C0, (403) 762-3777; or the Lake Louise Visitor Centre, (403) 522-3763.

Long ago when Sun was ruler of Earth, Water approached Sun to ask for a little of his great power. Sun agreed. But Water took more than Sun intended. Laughing and dancing, Water proceeded to sculpt the mountains, tear down the cliffs, and flood the land. Sun became jealous and turned away from Earth.

Unexpectedly, water froze, her power locked in great frozen rivers of ice. Slowly, over eons, water built up her strength once again. She accumulated in high mountain glaciers. There, she continued to smooth down the mountains, albeit more slowly. Seeing that Water had once again outwitted him, Sun was amused

and smiled upon Earth. Free at last, Water tumbled down, creating numerous waterfalls and babbling streams. However, Sun turns his face away each year to remind Water that he can freeze her into slow-moving ice.

Though the land was carved by ice, Sun rules the Earth.

What Natives Call Themselves

Blackfoot tribe	Soyi-tapi	real people
Siksika	Sik sikah'	black moccasins
Blood	Kainai	many chiefs
Peigan	Aputoksi-pikuni	north people
Sarcees	Tsotli'na	earth people
Stoney	Assinipwat	stone people
Cree tribe	Nahiawuk	precise people
Beavers	Tsattine	dwellers among beavers
Slavey	Acha'otinne	woodland people

Moraine Lake is typical of
the majestic scenery that can be
found in the Canadian Rockies. The
peaks that form the backdrop for the lake
are called the Wenkchemna Mountains—
"wenkchemna" means *ten* in Stoney.
Each of the peaks is named using
Stoney numbers from
one to ten.

LUXTON MUSEUM: BANFF

Teepees, horses, weapons, and warbonnets are probably the most well-known symbols of native people anywhere. Hidden behind log fort-like walls, the Luxton Museum presents a number of static life-size displays. The scenes illustrate everyday life from the plains cultures at contact. Additionally, there are assortments of artifacts on loan from the Glenbow Museum, a number of artifacts contributed by private individuals, and two Charlie Biel dioramas. Interestingly, the taxidermist's life-size Cree "dog" team is made up of wolves.

Started in the 1950s by Norman Kenny Luxton, a resident of Banff, the museum was willed to the Glenbow Institute about 1961. It operated as a subsidiary of the Calgary-based museum until 1991. The Buffalo Nations Cultural Society purchased the facility in March 1992 and this not-for-profit association is now working on augmenting the existing exhibits.

The Buffalo Nations Cultural Society was established in 1989 to fomalize the alliance of individual natives from Treaty 7 tribes, including members from the Blackfoot (Siksika), Sarcee (Tsuu T'ina), Peigan (Aputoksi-pikuni), Blood (Kainai) and Stoney (Nakoda) nations. These people are also interested in establishing a more extensive Indian Cultural Park.

Group tours can be pre-booked; periodic dancing and craft-making demonstrations are held; phone for times. The museum is located west of the Bow River Bridge. The museum is anxious to note that it is in no way associated with the nearby Indian Trading Post. The Luxton Museum itself offers a selection of native arts and crafts, publications, and museum-quality reproductions. Information is available from the Luxton Museum, Box 850, 1 Birch Ave, Banff, AB T0L 0C0, (403) 762-2388.

Among the displays is a depiction of the Sundance ritual. Blowing a whistle made from an eagle bone and dancing to the drumbeat, a warrior's heroic endurance brought renewal to the land and to his tribe.

Banff Buffalo Nation Heritage Days

Held in August each year, the present festival is a lively affair, but pales in comparison to the extravaganzas held around the turn of the century. Originally organized in 1889 as a diversion to soothe railway guests stranded by bad weather, the original Banff Indian Days festival grew into a 50-or-more teepee encampment. Weeks of all-out competitions, presented by the Stoney Nation, included drumming, dancing, and horse-racing.

Over the years, an increase in the number of regional rodeos and other powwows diminished the effort until its demise in 1977. In 1992, a modest version of the festival was revived as an annual means of reviving the historic connection between Banff and its neighbouring native peoples.

Information is available from the Banff Chamber of Commerce, (403) 762-3777.

SUNDANCE LODGES:
KANANASKIS COUNTRY

Kananaskis Country is not as well-known as nearby Banff National Park. However, the same range, the Rocky Mountains, forms a spectacular backdrop for guests who wish to get sleepy in a teepee.

Surrounded by towering peaks, Kananaskis Country is a gateway through the Rockies. Located near the Kananaskis Lakes, a Visitor Centre explains the topography through features such as an interactive audio-visual presentation touching on the archaeological work done in the area before the highway was built. Information from the visitor centre is available from (403) 591-7222. Information on Kananaskis Country is available from Suite 412, 1011 Glenmore Trail SW, Calgary, AB T2V 4R6, (403) 297-3362. From December 1 through June 15, sections of Highway 40 are closed. Information on the road is available from Fortress Junction, (403) 591-7371.

The teepee is a practical and environmentally sound shelter first perfected by the natives of the plains and mountain cultures. These teepees-for-tourists are modified somewhat for modern comforts. Inside each unit is a bed with a foam mattress, a radiant heater, a lantern, towels, cooking utensils, bedding, and most importantly, an elevated floor. Outside each of the 24 teepees are a firepit and a grill, as well as a picnic table.

Wanting to share the fun of living in a teepee without all the discomforts, Sundance Lodges in Kananaskis Country also offers visitors hot showers, a laundry, and an on-site store. The operation is not native-owned. Sundance Lodges is accessible via the Beaver Pond turnoff along highway 40 in Kananskis Country. Information is available before May 1 from Box 1869 Claresholm, AB T0L 0T0, (403) 625-4100; after May 1, Box 190, Kananaskis Village, AB T0L 2H0, (403) 591-7122.

Nestled beside tranquil Chief Hector Lake in the Rocky Mountains, but outside the national park, the native-owned Nakoda Lodge was opened in 1981. The Goodstoney Tribe that operates the facility provides visitor services that are said to range in consistency. Some guests report a comfortable stay; others express concerns. Offering conference facilities, a large restaurant, and a Sunday brunch of renown, the lodge has 50 guest rooms. Nakoda Lodge is 30 km off Highway 1 and Highway 1A near Canmore. Information is available from the Nakoda Lodge, (403) 881-3949, (403) 881-3951, fax (403) 881-3901.

Special Tours: Departures from Banff and the Foothills

Anchor D Guiding and Outfitting, Box 656, Black Diamond, AB T0L 0H0, (403) 933-2867; by wagon, hay or sleigh rides; 1 to 3 days.

Covered Wagon Holidays, Box 221, Longview AB, T0L 1H0, (403) 933-3599; by covered wagon; 1 to 3 days.

Hunter Valley Recreational Enterprises, Box 1620, Canmore AB, T0L 0M0, (403) 678-2000; by canoe, 8-day guided tour; other packages.

Mirage Adventure Tours, Box 2338, Canmore, AB T0L 0M0, (403) 678-4919; by raft, bike, kayak, helicopter, or cross-country skis; guided 1- to 2-day tours.

Misty Mountain Outfitters, Box 1005, Nanton AB, T0L 1R0, (403) 470-0456 (Edmonton); by horse, 2- to 7-day backcountry trips.

Rocky Mountain Cycle Tours, Box 1978-1, Canmore, AB T0L 0M0, (403) 678-6770, fax (403) 678-4451; by bicycle, 6 days in the Rockies.

Rocky Mountain Raft Tours, Box 1771, Banff AB T0L 0C0, (403) 762-3632; by raft, 1-hour scenic float trips on the Bow river.

The Adventure Group, Suite 202, 1414 Kensington Road NW, Calgary AB, T2N 3P9, (403) 283-8446; by raft, 1 to 10 days on whitewater rivers.

Wilderness Cookouts, c/o 132 Banff Ave, Banff, AB, (403) 762-4551, fax (403) 762-8130; by horseback or horse-drawn carriage, 1-day mountain explorer tour with generous meals.

117

PASSING OF THE LEGENDS
MUSEUM: SEEBE

Built to hold 40 years of private gifts and memorabilia from native people, the barn-like museum is open to visitors.

The Rafter Six Ranch is open to visitors who enjoy horse riding, generous meals, log cabin comforts, and western hospitality. Stan Cowley, owner of the guest ranch, is a recognized "honourary white chief." From his active lifelong interaction with native people in the surrounding communities, he receives and gives many gifts.

To display more than 40 years of native memorabilia, he has constructed a barn-like building at his ranch. Open to the public, with or without staying at the ranch, Cowley's personal collection is best appreciated if he is available to act as the tour guide. Visitors first view a collection of peacepipes, then climb stairs to see photo-graphs of various chiefs. On display are buckskin clothing, dance figures, many objects of native pride, and a fully pitched teepee, complete with liner. The distinctively painted buffalo skulls are symbols of secret societies. In the back room are examples of blue Treaty Coats. When a treaty was signed, one of the North West Mounted Police would sometimes resurrect an old military jacket and an acquired hat. After sewing on new yellow stripes, the North West Mounted Police would present it to the chief during the ceremony. Natives wore the ill-fitting jackets partly out of pride and partly out of politeness.

Mounted on the walls are tomahawks and other implements of war. It is said that the secret weapon that kept the Blackfoot Confederacy victorious was the long lance.

In previous times, before an all-out battle, opposing native warriors would ride out to meet each other. Posturing, threatening, and waving their weapons menacingly, they could sometimes frighten the other side away without a blow being landed. In spite of the gestures, both sides used the opportunity to look over the other side's state of readiness — horses, warriors, and weapons. At these encounters, the Blackfoot brandished short lances, about 1.5 m long. On the other hand, groups that feared the fabled Blackfoot brought their best weapons in a sincere effort to frighten the fearsome enemy off. If the skirmish progressed to a real battle, the Blackfoot were prepared. A sharp bayonette tipped the Blackfoot long

lance— a weapon about 3 m long. These spears easily dislodged a mounted man armed with a shorter lance. Because of the carnage typical of these battles, no one lived to tell tales. The Blackfoot were able to keep their long lances secret for a very long time.

Plains natives have successfully captured the popular imagination: mounted warriors and feathered buffalo hunters have become legendary, inspiring countless

novels and movies.

In addition to the museum, there is a log cabin restaurant on site. The Passing of the Legends Museum is located near Exshaw, west of Calgary and east of Canmore. There are signs on TransCanada Highway 1 indicating the turn-off. Information is available from Rafter Six Ranch Resort, Seebe, AB T0L 1X0, (403) 673-3622, (403) 264-1251, fax (403) 673-3961.

Chief Chiniki Restaurant and Handicraft Centre: Morley

This native-owned centre is located on a reserve just off Highway 1. The handicraft area offers a large selection of hand-made typical native crafts from Alberta. Many items are produced locally by members of the Stoney tribes, the Chiniki, Bearspaw, and Goodstoney bands.

Also on display, and some-times for sale, is a collection of beaded dance costume acces-sories. These showcases give visitors a chance to view the intricate hand work that goes into each dance item.

In the same building, buffalo

and bannock are the specialties at the modest café. Besides regular fare, such as bacon-and-egg breakfasts, the menu offers buffalo steak, buffalo stew, muskox stew, venison stew, and the all time favourite—buffalo burgers. Some of these dishes are available only in season.

The centre is located on the side of TransCanada Highway 1 at Morley, west of Calgary. It can be seen from the highway; there are signs. Information is avail-able from Chiniki Restaurant and Handicraft Centre, Box 190, Morley, AB T0L 1N0, (403) 881-3748, (403) 881-3960.

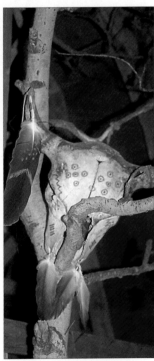

Said to possess great powers, painted skulls are used as symbols by secret societies.

PEOPLE OF THE BUFFALO

In the vastness of the tall prairie grasses there were no fences, no railroad tracks, no signs. Buffalo roamed as they desired. Today, telltale signs of human settlement encroach on the last untouched stretches.

The pre-contact lifestyle of the nomadic teepee-dwelling tribes of the plains are well-known through popular literature. In Alberta today, the main tribal groupings speak variations from three linguistic groups: Algonquin, Athapaskan, or Siouan-Assiniboine. Many tribal histories are under revision as further research continues into their oral traditions.

At contact, the Blackfoot Confederacy, along with the Apaches and Comanches far to the south, attracted great admiration for their prowess in war. Because the Confederacy was up to the challenge of resisting newcomers in war engagements, bureaucrats in eastern Canada quickly learned it was to their advantage to negotiate, rather than

fight. Known today as the Blood, Peigan, and Siksika, their language is Algonquian. In previous times, the Blood were distinguished for training the greatest warriors. However, all Blackoot Nations were adept in war.

The Sarcee, who hold lands near present-day Calgary, are also proud of their warlike reputation. From time to time, they affiliated with the Blackfoot tribes. However, they also argued with them. It is said that they held their own in these altercations. Descended from an Athapascan linguistic tradition, the Sarcees are an offshoot of the more northern Beaver nations.

The Stoney are part of the

Mokokit-ki-ackamimat means be "wise and persevere."
—Blackfoot, proverb

much larger Sioux Nation to the south. However, long before contact, they became allies of the Cree and the enemy of many Sioux brothers. Also known as the Assiniboine, the ever-mobile Stoney were the first to obtain guns from the Hudson's Bay Company in about 1670, on the shores of Lake Winnipeg. So armed, they pressed a wedge between the Gros Ventre and the Blackfoot to the south and the Beaver to the north. Eventually, they settled in the eastern shadow of the Rocky mountains, where they remain today.

The Cree are one of the largest tribes in Canada,

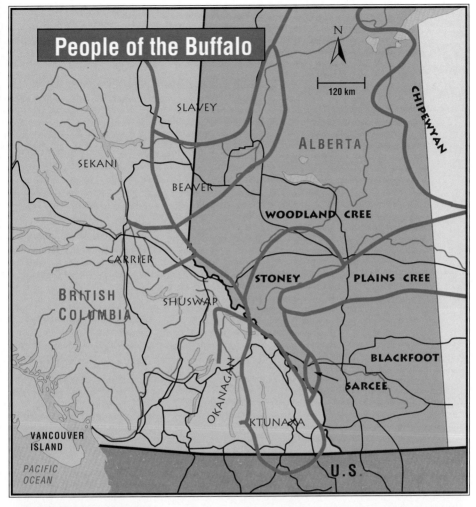

People of the Buffalo

N

120 km

SLAVEY

ALBERTA

CHIPEWYAN

SEKANI

BEAVER

WOODLAND CREE

CARRIER

STONEY

PLAINS CREE

BRITISH COLUMBIA

SHUSWAP

BLACKFOOT

SARCEE

OKANAGAN

KTUNAXA

VANCOUVER ISLAND

PACIFIC OCEAN

U.S.

Modern Siksika Woman

Originally from the prairies, Sandra White is currently Coordinator of the Native Tourism Development Program at the Native Education Centre in Vancouver, and a Director of the First Nations Tourism Association. She believes it is important for natives to share their culture with visitors, but at the same time to have control over what they share. Sandra is attuned to the special approach native people take towards business.

"Unlike other business owners," says White, "it is equally important that native people involved in cultural

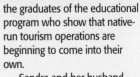

tourism initiatives discharge their responsibilities to their community." White is gratified by

the graduates of the educational program who show that native-run tourism operations are beginning to come into their own.

Sandra and her husband also own an outdoor adventure tour company based in British Columbia that specializes in fishing and getaway packages. Information is available from Inside Passage Adventures, (604) 875-6751.

Stoney Chief

having groups extending from Hudson Bay to the foot of the Rockies. They have always considered themselves to be enemies of the Blackfoot. Of the many Cree tribes that are recognized today, the Plains Cree occupy the central part of Alberta, and the Woods Cree, the north. Originally from the Algonquin linguisitic tradition, they call themselves Nahi-awuk, "the precise people." When buffalo herds were prevalent, the Cree travelled in large organized bands. They were famous for hunting on horseback, even killing buffalo in deep snow. They were also adept at acquiring horses from neighbouring bands. Well-known as intermediaries, they prospered by carrying furs between tribes and fur-trading forts. They are the group responsible for separating the Sarcees from the Beaver by settling between them.

The Chipewyan now occupy the northeastern corner of Alberta. Originally a northern people, they are adept at surviving in areas where there are caribou instead of buffalo. They often hunted caribou from canoes, killing the animals as they crossed a waterway. Their social structure was simple; the head of the family was respected. In previous times, other nations implied they were part-man, part-animal because they fashionably left the tails on their skin shirts. At contact, they were the enemies of the Inuit and made the decision to avoid white fur traders when

possible. In previous times, they established a series of uneasy truces with the Cree. Do not confuse these people with the Chippewas, a large tribe to the east around the Great Lakes.

The Beaver and the Slavey are from the Athapaskan linguistic tradition. They obtained their first guns about 1782. Thus armed, they stopped a Cree invasion and drove the unarmed Sekanis to the west of the Rockies. During the 1800s, many trading posts were built exclusively to do business with the Beaver and Slavey nations. While these natives were adept at negotiating with fur company employees, the Beaver abhorred any relationship between their women and whites. They once burned down a Hudson's Bay Company (HBC) post to protest such an incident. In response, the HBC closed all the posts that relied on their trade. First, they repossessed all the traps they could. Next, they refused to

Saskatoon Berries

The taste of saskatoon berries is described as a cross between blueberries and almonds. Found abundantly on sunny knolls across the prairies, ripe clusters were harvested. With a stone maul, they were pulverized along with dry buffalo meat, other game, and fats, plus other ripe berries, such as chokecherries. This produced a rich dried food called pemmican. In previous times, natives traded dry rolls of this foodstuff with fur traders, or used it themselves when fresh game was scarce.

Racing along on their mounts, young men rushed in unchallenged freedom over the plains.

sell gunpowder. Finally, they told the natives to walk 325 km to the nearest trading post. In only a few years, the HBC

Different Terms: Same Meaning

There is a variation in the usage of certain terms between Canada and the United States.

Certain terms are confusing; others use different words for the same entity.

Canada	United States
Algonkins (the people)	Algonquin (the language)
Blackfoot, Siksika	Blackfeet
Chipewyan	(confused with) Chippewas
Déné, Slavey	Slaves
Inuit, Eskimo	Eskimo
Ojibway, Ojibwa	Chippewa, Salteaux, Soto
Peigan, Piikani	Piegan, Pikuni
Sarcee, Tsuut'ina	Sarci
Stoney	Sioux, Assiniboine
band, people, nation	tribe, band
bannock	fry-bread
bison, buffalo	buffalo
native, aboriginal, First Nations	native-American, Indian
prairie, plains	plains
reserve, band lands	reservation
teepee or tipi	tipi, tepee, or tipee
trading post	(confused with) fort
wapiti, elk	elk
saskatoon berry	service berry

regretted the folly of their actions. The Beaver cheerfully went back to a traditional bow-and-arrow lifestyle and the Hudson's Bay Company noted a shortfall of more than 20,000 skins in a single season. After only three years, HBC quietly re-opened the posts.

Today, the Slavey people of northwestern Alberta prefer to be called the Déné or Dene Nation. Although similiar in habits to the Beaver, in previous times they avoided barren areas, preferring the woodland lifestyle. They were adept at ice-fishing and net fishing, as well as hunting moose and caribou. They are noted for traditional clothing that is highly decorated with dyed porcupine quills or beads and fringes.

In Alberta today, there are also scatterings of Ojibwa, Iroquois, Gros Ventre, Shoshoni, K'tuuaxa, and Crow native groups.

123

THE BUFFALO: STAPLE OF LIFE

The buffalo herd is subdued today, but its spirit is forever linked with the earth and to the vitality of native people themselves.

To late 19th century hunters both native and non-native, the buffalo represented profit from fertilizer bone-meal and buffalo robes. To native people on the land, the buffalo represented food, shelter, and clothing.

For eons, while buffalo were abundant, plains nomads used their body parts for most implements. Even dried dung served as fuel on the treeless plains. However, it is incorrect to portray prairie natives as dependent upon the buffalo for food. Pronghorn antelope, elk, prairie chickens, waterfowl, and small game were all found in great numbers. This was supplemented by many kinds of berries, notably saskatoons and chokecherries, as well as roots and tubers. While the southern plains people disdained fish as a matter of principle, northern woodland groups used fish to supplement their diets. It was the total anatomy of the buffalo that proved indispensable.

The figure of a mounted native hunter separating out an enraged buffalo for slaughter is a popular image, based somewhat on fantasy. In the days before rifles, spears were more effective than arrows, but buffalo are large animals, up to twice the size of domestic cattle and more athletic. A single hunter was at a great disadvantage.

Before the arrival of the horse and the repeating rifle, buffalo were mainly hunted by stealth. For weeks, the herd was coaxed across the prairie, then herded into compounds or stampeded over cliffs. Buffalo compounds were box canyons or fenced-in areas where the

> *Teach my children white man's cunning for two or three years, but let me follow the buffalo-hunting ways of my fathers.*
> —Spoken by the son of a Cree chief, 1857

Buffalo Viewing Areas: Alberta

Buffalo are no longer an endangered or threatened species, though certain species are challenged by diseases. They can be viewed at the following Alberta locations. Information is available from Alberta Tourism, 1-800-661-8888, (403) 427-4321.

Gilbertson Buffalo Paddock.................Amisk
Bison Trail...Drumheller
Elk Island National Park ....Edmonton
Wood Buffalo National Park.................Fort Chipewyan

buffalo could be confined until they were slaughtered. After slaughter, offerings were made to thank the creatures. Then a moon cycle or more was spent drying the meat for use between hunts.

Whatever quantity of buffalo was slain in previous times, a staggering number were killed in only a dozen years beginning in 1872. Prior to that time, early travellers spoke of millions of buffalo as far as the eye could see. Conservative estimates place the number at about 60 million. By 1885, after the onset of commercial hunting, the herds were gone. In the year 1875 alone, more than 500,000 buffalo skins were shipped to Montreal, a distribution point. They were popular as sleigh blankets, to cover horses, and as military

Native Stoney woman with a child in a travois

greatcoats. In order to acquire modern technology for their people, Métis and native groups came under enormous pressures to obtain currency to buy goods. This was most easily accomplished by selling buffalo robes and bones. To hunt buffalo for profit was logical for the advancement of their well being and that of their communities.

As the buffalo were depleted, the hot, dry summers and the long, cold winters took their toll. Big game became more scarce and the people relied more heavily on wild vegetable foods. These required more energy to collect than game meat. Starvation among prairie aboriginals became a reality. The afflictions historically associated with this sad period are devastating diseases and alcoholism. For all intents, aboriginal people have recovered from these scourges today, but the reputation of that moment in history persists in textbooks and in stories.

The Non-food Products of the Buffalo

Hide with hair .... floor coverings, beds, clothing, moccasins
Hide, no hair, soft .... clothing, mocassins, teepees, baby blankets
Hide, no hair, stiff .... quivers, parfleches, rigid containers
Bladders .... waterproof bags
Brains and Liver .... products to tan leather
Stomach .... cooking pots, watertight carriers
Bones .... scrapers, knives, awls, arrow shafts
Rib bones .... sleigh runners used as children's toys
Skull .... ceremonial objects
Horns .... cups, spoons, gunpowder flasks
Sinews .... bowstrings, threads, lashing cords, ropes
Tail .... fly-whisk
Hair .... stuffing, paintbrushes, ornaments, cords
Teeth .... necklaces
Dewclaws .... rattles
Hooves .... glue
Dung .... fuel

DWELLING TYPE: THE TEEPEE

Three teepees reflect the conical form that is said to be a conduit between the spirit realms of the sky and the natural realms of earth.

Several aboriginal peoples around the world developed a form of conical shelter: the Sami (Lapps) in Finland, the Yukaghir in Siberia, the Inuit in Labrador, the aboriginals in California. All these tents have a central fire, a smoke opening, an entrance that normally faces east, and a place of honour opposite the door. But while these traits are shared on the prairies, the plains teepee is not strictly conical in shape, but a tilted creation, steeper at the back. Also, true teepees

Opposite: Like a range of white mountains, several teepees stand powerfully on a carpet of sun-warmed prairie grass.

have adjustable flaps to regulate drafts, and interior hanging liners that act as insulators.

The migration of the buffalo determined the journeys of the people. Packing and repacking their teepees and possessions in good weather, they settled during the coldest part of the winter. But in spring, after first pausing for annual renewal ceremonies, bands would start their move. The ceremonies took place at large encampments where

> *The old Indians say there is no power in a square house, that they lost all their power when they gave up the round house.*
> —Reginald Laubin, white man at a teepee encampment, 1938

teepees were pitched in a semi-circle, leaving the central area open for the rituals.

The device used to transport goods and teepees was the dog and travois. A travois consisted of two long poles — teepee poles — hitched to a dog's sides. A webbed frame for holding the baggage was fastened between the poles. A family might own several dogs to move their possessions; important families owned up to 50 dogs. After the introduction of the horse, the travois device was adapted for the larger animal.

THE TEEPEE: COMMON SENSE

There are several common sense rules associated with teepee life that may not be apparent to those who have never lived in a teepee.

East of the Rockies, the prevailing winds are westerly, so smoke flaps are most effective when the door faces east. Women have the last say on the exact orientation. In regard to firewood, not every type is suitable for an indoor fire. Dogwood burns with a stinky smell; evergreens give off too much smoke; fir wood throws out sparks. Since there are several buffalo robes spread about, spitting fires are not appreciated. Alder wood burns hot and is odourless. During conversation, a handful of sweetgrass may be added to the fire to give the interior a pleasant smell.

There is much protocol within teepee encampments. When pitching camp, elders have the first choice of position. Not all teepees are painted, only those of powerful families. When visiting with friends, there are several rules. If the door is open, all may enter. If the door is closed, a visitor calls softly, then waits. If the visitor is a close friend, the door might be rattled. A person who does not want company coughs softly. Lovers sometimes arrange secret signals barely audible through the thin walls. If a family is away, or if they do not wish company, they either fasten the door tightly or cross two sticks in front.

In previous times, the

The teepee is a symbol of an era when a nomadic lifestyle on the open prairie was a way of life.

teepee was the wife's domain. Furs and blankets were piled up invitingly, and the comfort level improved greatly with the use of ingeniously designed backrests. There was an altar area. Furnishings were mainly used by the men, but made, packed-up, and "owned" by the women.

Generally, the men sat separately from the women. The elders, sons, and guests used the backrests. On entering a teepee, guests and their families moved to their designated areas around the outside circumference. If passing between a person and the central fire, the intruder asked for pardon from each person.

At a feast, the men were served first; at all-male gatherings, the young men served the older men. During gatherings, the guests ate first — before the host began to eat — and guests were encouraged to take leftovers home. Guests brought their own utensils and knives. Only one category of resident ignored protocol. Early traders reported that on some mornings, the dogs burst into the tents, panting and stomping on sleeping bodies with no regard to order.

Teepee liners were essential furnishings. Not only did they provide insulation against the winds, they also prevented shadows on the outside teepee

After contact, there was a short-lived attempt to get native people to live in permanent wooden "teepees." Instead of their regular well-lit dwellings, the new habitations were dark and quickly became stale inside. They were immovable and prone to catch fire. They were not popular.

walls. When a fire is lit in the interior and there is no liner hanging inside, the shadows of the people are clearly visible. This was tempting for enemies who could identify people by their shadows. Liners were always hung in place.

Unlike the stark interior of teepees in movies and on television, plains teepees were colourful, with painted liners. They were furnished with backrests, piles of furs, buffalo robes, blankets, and bundles of goods. Most of all, they were warm with good companionship.

A Camera Safari: Teepees in Alberta

Teepees, in use.............................Annual powwow festivities
Indoor teepee ....Luxton Museum, Banff
Indoor teepee ....Passing of the Legends, Seebe
Teepees, summer only................Stoney Indian Park, Morley
Teepees, for rent...........................Sundance Lodge, Kananaskis
Teepees, inside a fort....................Fort Museum, Fort Mcleod
Indoor Teepee ....Museum, Head-Smashed-In
Teepee, outside a fort..................Indian Battle Park, Lethbridge
Indoor teepee ....Glenbow Museum, Calgary
Outdoor teepee............................Heritage Park, Calgary
Indoor teepee ....Sarcees Peoples Museum, Calgary
Indoor teepee ....Provincial Museum, Edmonton
Teepee monument, metal.........Saamis Teepee, Medicine Hat

Information is available from Alberta Tourism, 1-800-661-8888, or (403) 427-4321.

BELIEF SYSTEMS: PLAINS PEOPLE

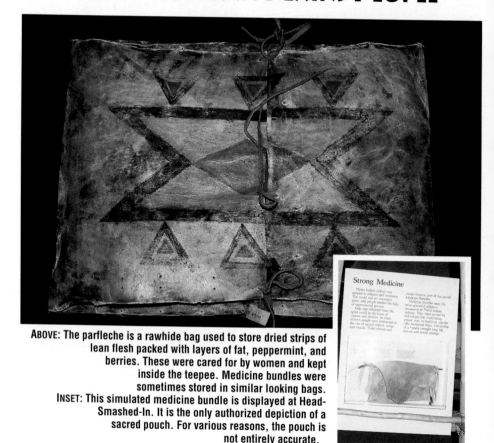

Strong Medicine

ABOVE: The parfleche is a rawhide bag used to store dried strips of lean flesh packed with layers of fat, peppermint, and berries. These were cared for by women and kept inside the teepee. Medicine bundles were sometimes stored in similar looking bags.
INSET: This simulated medicine bundle is displayed at Head-Smashed-In. It is the only authorized depiction of a sacred pouch. For various reasons, the pouch is not entirely accurate.

The native people of the prairies share similar, but not identical, spiritual beliefs. The great sacred figures are the Sun, the Thunderbird, and Napi, a trickster spirit-man of variable powers.

In previous times, all adolescents were expected to complete an initiation. Girls were isolated until they received a vision and a song. Boy's rituals were more elaborate. Each boy used this period to prove he could confront danger and protect his people from hostile outsiders. The more bravery he showed, the greater his later honours in life. During a boy's initiation and vision quest, a guardian spirit would transmit a song and a dance to him, plus give him amulets and other objects to make him powerful.

Over time, spiritual objects that were found to be especially powerful were placed in a medicine bundle. These packages were prepared and renewed by holy men, but often hidden away by the women. The power of a tribal family was bound up with the efficacy of their secret objects. An elder might lend a warrior one of these special objects, particularly a powerful feather, before going into battle. Some bundles had names and were widely renowned. During raids, enemies tried to locate and capture medicine bundles.

Purification was a life-long process—enhanced by the dark and steamy interior of a sweat lodge. New initiates went through long fasts and ceremonies at these lodges. Older people enjoyed simpler, shorter sweats.

Plains people also elaborated a role for secret societies, groups of like-minded men or women who banded together to control various rituals. These societies called the timing of the hunts, knew the movements of the herd, choreographed the Sun Dance, and called for war. One women's society was called Motokik; the men participated in several societies.

The most sacred of all ceremonies was the Sun Dance—held late summer in a special lodge covered with leafy branches. The Blackfoot ceremony honoured Sacred Woman, a entity who could renew the world. With the help of her son Scarface, and through her marriage to Morning Star, she had the power to obtain the sacred elements of renewal. Most provoking of the Sun Dance ceremonies was the ceremonial climax, an act of self-mutilation by a brave warrior.

Other ceremonies were integrated into the passing of the seasons. For the long winter nights, societies organized story-times. These continuing tales imparted information on why the world was created, a person's responsibilities, the secrets of animals, and why youngsters need to show respect.The medicine man or shaman was a person prone to having visions from an early age. A combination of beating

> *You stand up; you utilize me. You untie me: I am powerful.*
> — Blackfoot, Chant of the Medicine Bundle

drums, fasts, and sweats carried the shaman to another world where he or she sought the answers to important questions: how to heal a disease, how to rectify an imbalance. Occasionally, the questions were simple, such as "Who is gossiping about the chief?" Sacred plant hallucinations are part of the shamanistic tradition to the present day. However, no shaman ever takes a substance for pleasure. He or she journeys to another reality, all the while working hard for the answer to puzzling questions.

Among plains groups the chief and shaman , or medicine man, were different people. By contrast, among the coastal people these two functions were usually carried out by the same person.

Alberta Visitor Information

Information about native experiences, travel information, accommodation guides, and roadmaps are available from Alberta Tourism, 10155 102 St, Edmonton, AB T5J 4L6, (403) 427-4321, toll-free in North America 1-800-661-8888, fax (406) 427-0867, United States office, (212) 759-2222, Great Britain office, 44-71-491-3430, Japan office, 81-3-3475-1171.

Displaying Sacred Items

Among the Blackfoot, medicine bundles are considered among their most sacred artifacts. Exhibiting these items is a complicated issue. In 1987, before the opening of the Head-Smashed-In Interpretive Centre, Peigan elders undertook long discussions regarding the display and interpretation of such items. Some felt it was profane to display them. Others felt it would be unfair not to portray them since they are an essential part of the Blackfoot religion. In the end, the Peigan elders agreed to assemble a simulated medicine bundle, one made to look the same from the outside, but empty inside. Unlike authentic bundles, it is not renewed annually and the sign on it indicates that it is a replica. Elders from the nearby Blood Band continue to object to any public exhibit of sacred bundles.

The photograph pictures a regalia bag. Used to store items, such as pipes, or long feathers used during sacred ceremonies, it sometimes had its own tripod. The regalia bag was cared for by men and usually kept outside the teepee.

MEDICINE WHEELS: ALBERTA

ABOVE: A medicine wheel stands near this unusually coloured embankment, beside the fork of two rivers. Medicine wheels are often built in proximity to rivers or on hilltops.
INSET: When studying sacred circles, researchers paint the stones white to make them visible to low-flying aircraft. Only from the air is it possible to photograph a circle in its entirety.

Medicine wheels are the subject of several academic investigations, but their meaning continues to be debated. Found atop plateaus in southern Alberta, Saskatchewan, and Montana, there are about 150 surviving circles. Most are crowded within a 200-km radius of the confluence of the Red Deer and South Saskatchewan rivers. A medicine wheel is a group of sun-bleached boulders set in a circular pattern the size of several football fields. Some have spokes like a wagon wheel; others have prominent stone cairns; others radiate outwards like the sun; still others are made in the form of concentric circles. A few are made in the shape of turtles or people. About 135 of the wheels are built on similiar landscape features, including hilltops, and are in proximity to rivers or to buffalo jumps. The design most exclusively associated with the Blackfoot nation is the radiating sun design.

Since they were noticed by settlers about 150 years ago, several far-fetched explanations have been advanced. According to the wildest speculations, they were built by space aliens, Aztecs, mystical Hindus, wandering Phonecians, or gnomes. Some academics have commented that these theories are somewhat racist in viewpoint, since they all assume that early plains natives lacked the ability to express their ideas in rocks and circles. The fact that the plains natives still remember the reason for their existence, and continue to construct sacred circles, is

little acknowledged. Perhaps outsiders have a need to be confounded by them.

Many of North America's medicine wheels are as old as England's Stonehenge or Egypt's pyramids. This is one reason they have aroused much curiosity. Outsiders with less of a "space alien" orientation have naturally jumped to the calendar/sundial theory. However, investigations into the wheels have never uncovered a link between the wheels and seasonal or astronomical data.

In fact, the wheels were individually made and probably defy neat academic categories. Various wheels have various meanings, all within a specific range of probability and all deeply spiritual. Native people say that medicine wheels serve to commemorate the dead and to anchor spiritual observances.

To the present time, when a great chief or elder dies, their body is placed in a teepee and a large memorial of circular stones erected around it. Over time, the teepee and body disappear, leaving the memorial. There have been ancient remains located around the cairns or at the centres of certain wheels.

Other circles were used as ceremonial places. One wheel was known to be the place of rain dances, invoking the Creator to use Thunderbird to send rain. Thus some of the wheels may mark the location of spiritual ceremonies. Also in previous times, for spiritual observances, about one-third of the wheels probably had a central wooden pole that cast a shadow onto the surrounding spokes. As the shadow moved it was possible to speak with various deities, or it was time to pray. Early Christian missionaries report that devout Blackfoot people, practising their own religion, prayed more often than they did.

One further purpose is reported for the wheels. Enemies who encountered the stones were immediately reminded that they were in someone else's territory. The great stone circles served to frighten them off.

ABOVE: Sundial Hill Medicine Wheel

Listen, the Stones are Speaking

An archaeological site often contains fragmentary evidence of past cultures. For more information about archaeology in Alberta, or for joining an archaeological dig, contact the Archaeological Society of Alberta, Calgary Centre, 3624 Cedarille Drive SW, Calgary, AB T2W 3X8; the Strathcona Archaeological Society, 14716 - 65 Street, Edmonton, AB T5A 2D1; or the Alberta Underwater Archaeological Society, Box 113, Medicine Hat, AB T1A 7E8. For information on medicine wheels, contact the Archeological Survey of Canada, 8820 - 112 Street, Edmonton, AB T6G 2P8.

TRADING POSTS AND FORTS: SOUTHERN ALBERTA

Fort Whoop-Up was massive; it was surrounded by a 5-metre stockade topped by sharpened stakes. The doors, windows, and chimneys were barred with iron. There were two corner bastions and two cannons. In the years between 1872 and 1874, the fort served as the headquarters for Dave Akers and his men, a rag-tag band of Confederate Army veterans who sold whiskey to the natives.

When a group of Hudson's Bay Company fur traders learned that the whiskey fort was armed with cannons and that Aker's Blackfoot warrior friends numbered 2,000, they sent an urgent message to Ottawa. By February 1874, about 100 new recruits, along with their horses and wagons formed into a military unit and set out for Fort Whoop-Up. After marching 1300 km and meeting with several disasters, the division found itself hopelessly lost. Under the guidance of Métis Jerry Potts, they found their way to the whiskey fort.

Arriving at Fort Whoop-Up, the tired commanders accepted an invitation to dinner with the Americans. The conversation must have been interesting. The Americans fled without incident the following day. Jerry Potts, the indispensible guide, stayed with the force another 22 years. He was buried with full military honours.

In late 1876, after the U.S.

Today the Northwest Mounted Police are more commonly known as the Mounties. The blue coats, pictured on the right, were sometimes presented to a chief upon the signing of a treaty.

7th Cavalry fiasco at Little Big Horn, a band of 4,000 Sioux led by the fearless Sitting Bull, arrived in the region. They lived under Canadian protection for four years. However, with the buffalo gone, under threats from the Blackfoot Confederacy, and of his own volition, Sitting Bull and his people changed their minds and surrendered to the U.S. military in 1880. The massacre of those same natives at Wounded Knee occured some years later.

Unlike the American experience, the Mounties were a quasi-military unit formed ostensibly to protect the natives—not to vanquish them. The Mounties went on to occupy several forts throughout Saskatchewan and Alberta.

A full-sized model of Fort Whoop-Up and an interpretive centre is open to the public in Lethbridge, AB, (403) 329-0444.

Native Interactions: Alberta Tourist Attractions

These tourist attractions derive part of their content from a historical interaction with native people.

Fort Museum..Fort Macleod
Fort Whoop-Up Interpretive Centre....Lethbridge
RMH National Historic Park..................Rocky Mountain House
St. Paul de Cris Cairn.............................Brousseau
Kinosoo Totem Poles..............................Cold Lake
Cemetery Spirit Houses ....Rocky Lane
Indian Cabins and Tree Grave.............Old Mackenzie Highway

WHERE NATIVES GATHER: ALBERTA

The haunting strains of the old ways spiral around at powwows, soar into the sun-bleached sky, return to be grounded in the delicate footsteps of the dancers. There they are transformed into a living culture.

Long into the night, finishing touches are sewn onto elaborate costumes. The sleepless nights over, the costumes fastened, the public address system tested, the Grand Entrance ceremony finally begins. First, one of the elders reads the opening prayer, then the flags unfurl. Drums pound, the tension rises, and the parade ground swells as circles of dancers spiral into the grassy arena. From 300 to 800 dancers, each in their own type of costume and each with their own dance steps, enter the grounds. They come from throughout the United States and Canada. They come to compete in the all-native rodeo, to sell beadwork, jewellery, and T-shirts. They come to eat bannock. And mostly they come to dance, to hear the drums, and to greet friends they have not seen for a year. This is a powwow.

Many native people follow the powwow circuit, travelling from one event to the next during the busy June, July, and August season. The 1:00 p.m. parades are an important part of the celebration. Elders, women, young men, and youngsters, wear the finest regalia of their ancestors, or show off newly inspired costumes. Native princesses, from a dozen tribes are scattered throughout the procession. It is a dazzling sight. Each princess helps sell raffle tickets and raise money for her community.

Information is available from Alberta Tourism, 1-800-661-8888, (403) 427-4321.

To Contract A Professional Native Dance Group

Chadi K'azi, also known as Red Thunder Native Dance Theatre, operates under the direction of Lee Crowchild from the Tsuu T'ina Nation, Calgary. The company's dancers are chosen from nations throughout western Canada. Formed in 1987, the troupe presents traditional dances in theatrical settings. The professional choreography is highlighted by authentic costumes, feathers, buckskins, bells, and beaded jewellery. One of the troupe's most energetic presentations is the famous Hoop Dance, a spirited dance originating among the Hopi of the American southwest desert.

Chadi K'azi has appeared on stage in California, New York, Alaska, across Canada, and parts of Europe. The troupe is booked up to a year in advance. Information is available from Red Thunder Native Dance Theatre, c/o Boxer Productions, 622A Edmonton Trail NE, Calgary, AB, (403) 230-0331.

NATIVE PARTICIPATION IN THE STAMPEDE: CALGARY

The Calgary Exhibition and Stampede, touted as the "Greatest Outdoor Show on Earth," is noted for its top professional cowboys. What is not as well known is that many of those "cowboys" are native people who have risen to become world class bronco riders, calf ropers and bull riders.

The stampede is a fast-moving spectacle. Set against the hoopla of rodeo activity, native people make their own unique contribution. With quiet dignity, the Stoney and other native bands have participated in the opening parade for many years. They use the opportunity to show off their costumes and ride their finest horses. Additionally, they erect a teepee village, a group of teepees in which they live during the festivities.

Immediately following the late afternoon and evening Chuck Wagon races, there are stage shows and musical productions. From time to time, native dancers are asked to contribute to the evening's entertainment line-up.

Though the Stampede crackles with excitement, glitters with sequins, and offers an impressive array of livestock and cowboy competition skills, it is the native people that many visitors come to see. The soothing drumbeat in their teepee village is an indication of the heartbeat of the people. In their bells and buckskins, with their costumes

Native people add a vibrant component to the Stampede, adding to its overall appeal with their colour and energy.

and feathers, perhaps it is their vibrant component and their continued blessing that makes this specatacle so popular.

Information is available from the Calgary Exhibition and Stampede, Box 1860, Calgary, AB T2P 2M7, (403) 261-0101, 1-800-661-1260, fax (403) 265-7197.

136

Arts and Crafts: Calgary and Area

Whether machine-made or completely hand-made, moccasins are ideal for treading softly through the mist of an early morning. With silent footsteps, it is possible to hear the first bird songs that greet the dawn.

Native Arts: Calgary and Area

Chief Chiniki Handicraft Centre, Box 190, Off Highway 1, Morley (403) 881-3960

Cottage Fine Arts, 6503 Elbow Drive SW, Calgary (403) 252-3797

Eskimo Point Art, Palliser Hotel, 133 - 9 Ave SW, Calgary (403) 234-0990

Glenbow Museum Giftshop,130 - 9th Ave SE, Calgary (403) 268-4100

Indigenous Images, 454 Cannington Close SW, Calgary (403) 251-3826

International Native Arts Festival, Box 502, Calgary Held annually in August (403) 233-0022, fax (403) 233-7681

New Image Gallery, Suite 10, 1305 - 33rd Street NE, Calgary (403) 248-5355

Peigan Crafts and Peiganworks Moccasins, Box 100, Brocket (403) 965-3755

Rocky Barstad Bronze Sculptures, High River (403) 652-4303

Studio West Ltd, 205 - 2nd Ave SE, Cochrane (403) 932-2611

Unisource Art Gallery, 4247 Bow Trail SW, Calgary (403) 246-7800

Webster Galleries, 919a - 17 Ave SW, Calgary (403) 245-5747

Westlands Gallery, 118 - 2nd Ave West, Cochrane (403) 932-3030

The Blackfoot received their name from their practise of colouring their moccasins with carbon from burnt prairie grasses. Beadwork clothing and tanned buckskin moccasins are two of the best examples of prairie crafts.

There are two types of tanning processes for leather; hand-tanning or commercial tanning. Moccasins created from home-tanned moosehide emit a pervasive smoky odour. They are for outdoor use, and may need to be stored outdoors as well. Hand-made or machine-made moccasins created from commercially tanned skins are softer and have a delicate leathery odour. Beads are applied by hand to both machine-made and hand-made moccasins. With carefully hand-done beadwork, all moccasins are fine examples of craftsmanship. With an added border of fur, they are warm, comfortable, and practical.

Since beads were first introduced as a trade good, native craftspeople have shown a flair for their use. There are two main pattern types—geometric and floral. Geometric patterns are considered more masculine and floral patterns more feminine. Geometric patterning is said to reach its apex among the Stoney people. The Cree are said to have evolved floral patterns to a high art. However, there has been a melding of the traditions and modern bead workers are experts at both types of designs.

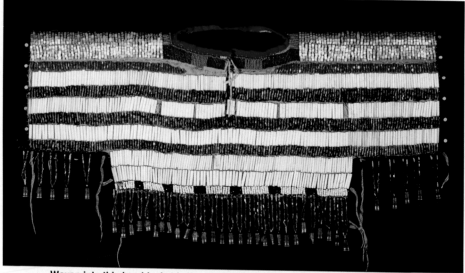

Woven into this bead jacket is the expansiveness of the prairie, the sparkle of the midday sun, and a hint of the fiery glory of the buffalo.

In previous times, Plains natives would embellish their clothes with dyed porcupine quills. The quills were flattened and laid into a pattern, then braided, woven, or plaited. The colours, obtained from roots and berries, were muted shades of yellow, mauve, beige, or light red. Most patterns were geometric in shape, rather like the zig-zag of needlework patterns.

After the introduction of trade goods, tiny seed beads became the preferred medium for decoration. Design work separated into two distinctive styles. Geometric patterns continued. They show ordered triangles, arrows, and mountain shapes, usually set against a white ground. However, the evolution of the floral shapes brought a rich, bright, new feminine style to the art.

The Woodland Cree, perhaps through exposure to Russian fur traders, first began experimenting with floral designs. In Slavic-like style, they designed brightly beaded flowers, stems, and leaves to flow over jackets and moccasins in a tangle of bright garden forms.

Today, geometric and floral traditions are practised together. Though they are rarely integrated into the same garment, the same bead workers are usually proficient at either type of design. Colours are vivid reds, blues, pinks, yellows, and blacks. The greatest examples of beadwork are reserved for entire costumes, such as those worn during powwows.

The artifacts in the Glenbow Museum's native collection range from Inuit clothing designed to withstand the harsh Arctic environment, to the elegant quillwork and beaded costumes of the natives of the plains. The Glenbow also displays an extensive collection of native artifacts and a permanent collection of art. Many of the art works have a native theme. The highlights of the art collection are 19th and 20th century watercolours, Inuit prints, and sculptures. Prominent artists include Jack Shadbolt, Emily Carr, and Carl Rungius.

As well as maintaining its permanent collection, the museum presents temporary theme exhibitions. In the recent past, there has been a tribute to the fur trade and a show of international beadwork. From time to time, there are guided tours of the facility; phone ahead.

In addition to the museum

and art gallery, the Glenbow also houses a library , an archival photographic collection, and archival material, including extensive holdings on native cultures. The Glenbow is a resource centre for researchers and students of history. The gift store at the museum carries a good selection of Canadiana: jewellery, posters, cards, books, top quality reproductions and native arts.

A guide to the museum is available in English or German. The museum is closed on Mondays. Information is available from the Glenbow Museum and Archives, 130 - 9th Ave SE, Calgary, AB T2G 0P3, (403) 268-4100, fax (403) 265-9769.

Tsuu T'ina Museum and Archives: Calgary

This museum, also known in tourist pamphlets as the "Sarcee Peoples Museum," is a small facility located inside a school on the Sarcee Reserve. The most noteworthy display item is a teepee liner, elaborately illustrated with Chief Bullhead's lifetime exploits. Something like a medieval tapestry, hundreds of figures interconnect on the painted piece. A guide is available to decipher the figures. Other displays include photographs, papoose boards, peace pipes, and assorted dance costumes.

Phone ahead to be certain the museum is open. Information is available from the Tsuu T'ina Museum and Archives, 3700 Anderson Road SW, Calgary, AB T2W 3C4, (403) 238-2677.

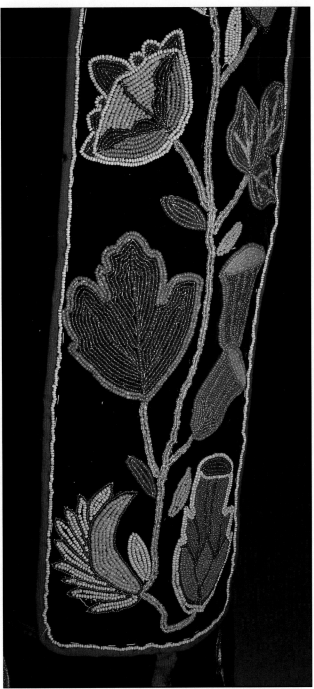

Some say Cree beadwork designs were influenced by Russian traders. Others say the touch of spring after the harsh winter was enough to inspire the artists who first created these rich floral designs.

WORLD HERITAGE SITE: HEAD-SMASHED-IN BUFFALO JUMP

ABOVE: The partially subterranean interpretive centre blends with the landscape and reflects the "hidden" nature of the jump. The jump site is to the right of this photograph.
INSET: Each sign, story, and display was composed after intensive deliberations with Peigan and Blackfoot elders.

At Head-Smashed-In Buffalo Jump, located in the Porcupine Hills of Alberta, an 11-metre high sandstone cliff looms up above a pile of bones approximately 12 m deep. In previous times, the cliffs were higher than they are today, not only because they were worn away from their use as a jump, but because the midden of bones has raised the level at the base. Evidence suggests that this particular jump was first used about 5700 years ago, and was last used about the year 1800.

After the arrival of the horse, buffalo jumps fell into disuse and many were looted by bone collectors. Fortunately, some of the sites remained undisturbed. This jump is one of the most spectacular and best preserved. Rather than leave the site as an archaeological curiosity, native and non-native individuals began working together about 1960 to develop it for public interpretation. The result is an architecturally designed, partially subterranean Interpretive Centre. State-of-the-art displays outline the history of the hunt and codify the stories of Napi, the creator of the Blackfoot people.

Native people were active throughout the development stages of the project. First, the field staff of the archaeological dig program were hired from the Peigan reserve. Later, teams of native people made the key judgments on all the displays and decided on the telling of their stories. The responses of millions of visitors to this Centre since its

Paved walkways to the jump site allow visitors to appreciate the scale of undertaking and the patience involved in stampeding an entire herd over the edge of the cliff.

arrows.

Visitors to the site will benefit by motoring the road behind the Interpretive Centre into the unusual hills. In these hills, archaeologists have discovered teepee rings, burial sites, rock alignments indicating drive lanes, and pits used to trap eagles for their feathers.

opening in 1987 clearly indicate that outsiders prefer stories told from the native point of view. Native people continue to work here and love the reward of presenting their own version of history. The site is preserved *in situ* for public education, as required under the conditions for a UNESCO World Heritage Site.

Buffalo jump sites such as this one were used in a communal fashion. Runners were sent out to find the animals. When they had located the herd, they spent the next few weeks coaxing the near-sighted animals up "drive lanes," mounds of stone indicating a path to the cliffs. As the days passed, men, women, and children would join in, slowly coaxing the animals forward. Finally, all members of the tribe joined together to create a great tumult. The beasts stampeded over the edge. There they were finished off with spears and

'Itsipa'k-sikkihkinihkoots si yao'pi' means "where he got his head smashed in."
—Peigan, name for this jump site

As well as displays, there are wheelchair accessible trails to the side of the jump, a film theatre with ongoing presentations, a gift shop and a cafeteria. Special lectures are periodically held; please inquire. A major powwow is presented on the site each July. Head-Smashed-In is located 18 km from Fort Mcleod on Highway 785. Information is available from Head-Smashed-In Buffalo Jump Interpretive Centre, Box 1977, Fort Macleod, AB T0L 0Z0, (403) 553-2731, (403) 265-0048, fax (403) 553-3141.

Small Native Artifact Collections: Southern Alberta

Museum and Art Gallery....................................Medicine Hat
East Irrigation District Museum...........................Scandia
Drumheller Fossil Museum, city centre...........Drumheller
Whyte Museum...Banff
Nose Creek Valley Museum...............................Airdrie
Tracey's Antiques Museum ....Hussar
Red Deer and District Museum ....Red Deer
RMH Museum ....Rocky Mountain House

Information is available from Alberta Tourism, 1-800-661-8888, (403) 427-4321.

BUFFALO JUMPS: SOUTHERN ALBERTA

This photograph shows one of the interpretive displays at Head-Smashed-In Buffalo Jump Museum. Head-Smashed-In is named after an unfortunate native youth who picked the wrong moment to stand under the jump.

Buffalos skulls are stacked high in this display. All parts of the bison were used by native hunters.

Prior to 1730 and the gradual introduction of the horse, tribes banded together to obtain buffalo. There were 60 million buffaloes on the plains before contact, but a person on foot had little chance against a whole herd. Buffalo jumps were more practical. Identified by mounds of buffalo bones, projectile points, and ceremonial objects, these jumps are located throughout the short grass plains.

Like a crack in a piece of drying clay, buffalo jumps are gigantic "cracks" in the flat prairie landscape. To be effective, a buffalo jump must be invisible from ground level; only the merest shadow betrays its presence. Called bluffs or coulees, these sudden, deep gulches are unique ledge-like formations that were put to good use.

The hunt was under the control of certain women and the secret society members who determined which strategies would be employed. For weeks in advance of a kill, native scouts wearing wolf costumes would gently usher the giant herd into the jump area. The process was slow and required many shifts of patient workers. Finally, when the herd was aligned, the

This buffalo jump, lying within Squaw Coulee, was discovered in 1952 when a flash flood bared bones and arrowheads at the base of a cliff. The story among the native people tells of men and women who lived in separate camps. The women were impatient with the men and constructed their own fences to funnel the herds onto the rocky ledge. Whenever a few buffalo wandered into the area, the women would leap up and yell, driving the beasts to their deaths. The story makes no mention of whether they shared their meat with the men.

Pis'kun means "deep blood kettle, or buffalo jump."
—Blackfoot

---

scouts and the people would stampede the animals over the cliffs, there to finish the animals off with arrows and spears.

After such an event, copious quantities of meat were sliced into thin strips and dried in the sun. Special flat skin-leather suitcases called parfleches were used to transport the meat. Anthropologists estimate that some buffalo jumps were used only once or twice per decade.

Head-Smashed-In Buffalo Jump Museum features interpretive displays that present the history of buffalo jumps in a vivid and dramatic fashion.

Buffalo Jumps and Attractions

Diorama of a Buffalo Hunt, Luxton Museum ....Banff
Head-Smashed-In Buffalo Jump and Museum ....Fort Mcleod
Mural of a Buffalo Jump ....High River
Old Women's Buffalo Jump Historic Site ....High River
Empress Buffalo Jump and Teepee Rings ....Empress
Dry Island Buffalo Jump Provincial Park....................Huxley and Elnora

Information is available from Alberta Tourism, 1-800-661-8888, (403) 427-4321.

WRITING-ON-STONE PROVINCIAL PARK: SOUTHERN ALBERTA

ABOVE: The best carvings are preserved in an area of hoodoos and sandstone cliffs found along an otherwise flat riverbed. From deep within the canyon walls, a shamanistic chord forever ricochets. The hushed spirit-chant climbs the lonely heights and is carried aloft on the gentle wind. INSET: Figures with upraised arms are characteristic and may have meaning within shamanistic practises.

T he Milk River rises in southwestern Alberta and northern Montana. It eventually joins the Missouri River and drains into the Gulf of Mexico. Because of its extensive drainage area, it has long formed a convenient corridor across the continent of North America. It was an important travel route for aboriginal people, and many native groups had occasion to pass through the area each season.

The river valley shows evidence of a rich archeological history. Several of the sandstone cliffs are covered with petroglyphs. Experts say the area was the centre for sacramental practises hinging on the perceived accessibility of spirits. Shamans and their initiates probably used the area for spiritual retreats. The earliest known rock art figures are believed to be Shoshoni, Assiniboine, and Gros Ventre, all forerunners of the Blackfoot who settled the area later.

The best carvings are preserved within Writing-on-Stone Provincial Park, an area of hoodoos and sandstone cliffs found along an otherwise flat river bed. All over the world, the survival of such carvings is dependent upon dry moisture levels and low bacterial activity. The environ-

ment here is ideal; the climate is desert-like and the soft sandstone is resistant to algae growths. Cave paintings in Germany, France, Spain, Belgium, Italy, and Great Britain are sometimes found in association with buried animal bones. Organic material can be carbon-dated and the paintings can then be accurately dated. Unfortunately, there are no organic deposits associated with these particular petroglyphs. However, experts say that similiar petroglyphs found elsewhere date to about 500 A.D.

The exact meaning of all of the petroglyphs has been lost in time. Since the Milk River was the site of vision quests,

many educated guesses have been made. The simplest mural depicts a battle between dozens of armed mounted warriors. Others depict a buffalo hunt, mountain goats, wapiti, and deer. Along the mythical line, the spirit of the horse is well represented, as are celestial birds that appear to be Thunderbirds. Many important human figures are depicted with upraised arms. Several drawings show a shamanistic preoccupation with the concept of transformation, skeleton figures with migrating hearts.

The semi-arid environment of the Milk River is popular with canoeists. Canoe season starts in April and continues into September. The

river is rated Class 1 for canoes, and is navigable for 385 km. An international water agreement between Canada and the United States regulates the amount of water in the river. While an acceptable level of water is usually kept in the system, there may be exceptional years; please inquire before planning a trip.

Writing-on-Stone Provincial Park is located 125 km southeast of Lethbridge on Highway 4. To view the petroglyphs on land, visitors must be accompanied by a tour leader. Daily guided tours depart regularly in summer. Information is available from Writing-on-Stone Provincial Park, Box 297, Milk River, AB T0K 1M0, (403) 647-2364; Chinook Country Tourist Association, 2805 Scenic Drive, Lethbridge, AB T1K 5B7, (403) 320-1222, 1-800-661-1222; or Milk River Raft Tours, Box 396, Milk River, T0K 1M0, (403) 647-3586.

Modern Storyteller

Brenda Andrews was raised in a non-native home, but always longed for her Cree roots. Now living on the coast, she works as a teacher's assistant helping other native children find their roots.

Andrews is a puppeteer, whose long journey back to her aboriginal home gave her life meaning. Through her puppet

workshops, offered to both adults and children, she shares native stories with people everywhere. "I like to bring out the child in everyone," she says. "Stories are the best way we can get our message across."

Native Legend Puppet Show performances can be booked, (604) 380-6818.

TEEPEE RINGS: CARMANGAY AND EMPRESS

ABOVE: Though these encampments have been long abandoned, the spirit of the ancestors is said to breathe at such places.
INSET: Teepee rings are colourations in the grass that indicate where early native people placed the rocks that held down the edges of their animal-hide tents.

Teepee rings are not medicine wheels. Teepee rings are marks left by the stones used by prehistoric peoples to hold down the edges of their skin tents. These early structures were made from a three- or four-post framework of lodgepole pine trunks, probably collected in the Rockies. To erect the shelter, the poles were first placed loosely in a circular position. A sewn form made from six to eight dehaired buffalo hides was laid over top. Then the poles were spread wide to tighten the skin. Two open flaps at the top drew smoke out of the lodge. The lower edge of the skin teepee was held down by large stones. When camp moved, the stones were left behind. They were re-used the next year when the group returned.

Nine semi-circular rings showing these marks are located at Carmangay. Today, they are merely discolourations in the grass. The area was a temporary base camp used for centuries during summer. Excavations have uncovered shards, broken tools, and scraps of buffalo bone. One arrowhead was discovered. The site was probably occu-pied for periods between 200 A.D. and 1700 A.D.

Carmangay is located on Highway 23, 20 km east of Claresholm. There is a road-side sign pointing out the site. Information is available from the Chinook Country Tourist Association, 2805 Scenic Drive, Lethbridge, AB T1K 5B7, (403) 320-1222, 1-800-661-1222.

A second interesting set of sites is located near Empress on Highways 41 and 562. There are teepee rings, a medi-cine wheel, and a buffalo jump. Information is available in the summer only from (403) 565-3983.

POWWOWS: SOUTHERN ALBERTA

Swirling, twirling people whirl in time to an ancient song to celebrate their culture. Participants alternate between spectating and taking part.

In previous times, ceremonial dancing was reserved for male warriors. Today, powwows are gatherings of both genders and all ages. From every corner of Alberta, Saskatchewan, and the northern U.S. states, native people follow the summer powwow circuit.

Powwow events are not put on for tourists. However, outsiders are welcome to attend, if they remember to leave their preconceptions behind. There really is such a thing as "Indian time," and visitors looking for prompt timing or sparking clean washrooms will be out of their comfort zone. Most of the time between dance competitions is spent walking around the fairgrounds, savouring a soft drink, deliberately digesting a hot dog, and accumulating layers of prairie dust.

Those who do appreciate the spectacle, will view a happy world. The feathers, singing, and drumming are relaxing to native people and they are usually at their least reserved. The elders appreciate the oneness of coming together and several ceremonies take place. There may be a public mourning for those who are gone, the giving away of blankets, and the bestowing of names. The public address system rarely works properly. The dance competitions go on and on. Late into the night young people continue to party.

Visitors who are looking for this unique experience should plan ahead. Do not trust scheduled dates. Powwows are rescheduled at the whim of the band. Call the nearest band office or Native Friendship Centre for last-minute confirmation.

Information is available from Alberta Tourism, 1-800-661-8888, (403) 427-4321. Ask for the separate "Powwow list."

Large Powwow Gatherings: Alberta	
Annual Powwow, Saddle Lake	June
Poundmaker Nechi Powwow, St. Albert	July
Alexis Annual Powwow, Glenevis	July
Indian Days and Powwow, Standoff	July
Buffalo Days and Tipi Village, Fort Macleod	July
Gathering of Nations, Bragg Creek	July
Powwow and Tipi Village, Head-Smashed-In	July
Peigan Nations Powwow, Brocket	July
Powwow, Lac La Biche	July
Ermineskin Cree Powwow, Hobemma	August

DANCES: NORTHERN PLAINS

Men's Traditional Dances evolved from the warrior rites of earlier times. Their circular back-tail attachments are called feather "bustles" and their headpieces, made from porcupine quills are known as "roaches." Some men's dance steps are an outgrowth of the Sneak-Up Dance. In this ancient dance, warriors act out the discovery of a wounded enemy. First approaching him cautiously, they suddenly swirl away in case he is still armed. Other dances approximate the actions of animals, such as the steps of the Crow Hop and the Rabbit Dance. There are two main categories of male dancers: Fancy Dancers and Traditional Dancers. Both use large body movements that blend up and down, head and eye movements with intricate spins, turns and twists.

The Men's Chicken Dance features elaborate regalia and equally complex dance steps. Some interpret the movements of this dance as derived from the puffed-up courtship instincts of a prairie chicken. By imitating the sensuous courting behaviour of the bird, the dance is said to serve the same function for humans. Throughout the 20th century, secondary costume details, such as ever-larger bustles, brighter colours, cosmic designs, variations of face paint, streamers on feather tips, and extra "roach feathers," have become increasingly popular. In response to this exuberance, a new type of dance classification was created, the New Fancy Dancer. They wear bright paint, fluorescent colours, up to three back bustles, arm bustles, and feathers that rotate. They dance with highly elevated foot and leg movements and a flourish of spins to attract attention. Part of their routine is to cease movement exactly as the last drum stops beating.

The rhythm of Grass Dancers is fundamentally an outgrowth of warrior dances, although many of the movements also imitate hunting actions. Said to have emanated from a vision of spirits rising like ghosts from the long prairie grasses, this dance has been adopted by many plains groups. In earlier times, long ropes of braided sweetgrass hung from the dancer's waists. Occasionally, a few long human hairs (or scalps) flowed from their shoulders and waists. Today, the outfits are constructed from brightly coloured yarns and the bustle is not present. In contrast to Fancy Dancers, Grass Dancers employ more swaying motions and deeper dips.

Jingle Dancers are a relatively recent addition to the dancing spectrum. Born of the vision of a sick woman who was healed, the Jingle Dance is considered therapeutic. Many dancers wear 365 bells to represent a prayer for each day of the year. Originally, the bells were made from snuff tobacco container lids. When Jingle Dancers appear as a group, their soft up and down movements are synchronized to create a pleasant jingle-in-unison sound resembling softly falling rain. Women dancers silently position their feet as light as feathers upon the wind. This reflects a deep respect for mother earth, in contrast to the men's vigorous styles.

PROVINCIAL MUSEUM: EDMONTON

The Provincial Museum in Edmonton recently opened a new gallery to showcase plains native heritage. Said to be one of the most comprehensive displays in Alberta, the new gallery is 900 sq m in area. Displays span the millennia, from the arrival of aboriginals in the New World, to the impact of the horse and contact with white settlers.

The first section of the new gallery is called "In All Their Finery." Featuring more than 100 representative pieces, it is a showcase of northern native life. The displays include a teepee, decorated clothing, and weapons. One unique exhibit is a full-size travois, the horse decked out in full regalia.

In another section of the gallery, there are informative displays on hide and bark, the uses of buffalo, and the assembly of porcupine quills into decorations for clothing. The natives' special relationship with nature is illustrated through their use of plants for healing.

Special performances, lectures, and films are held periodically; phone ahead. A cafeteria and a gift shop are on site. Information is available from The Provincial Museum of Alberta, 12645 - 102 Ave, Edmonton, AB T5N 0M6, (403) 453-9100; or recorded message, (403) 427-1786.

Inprevious times, clothing was made of hide and, for men, consisted of a shirt, breechcloth, leggings and moccasins. Women wore long dresses with their own leggings and moccasins. Decorations included such things as quillwork made from dyed porcupoine quills and rows of elk teeth on women's dresses. Tattoos were common; eagle feathers were occasionally worn in the hair. The long headdresses associated with plain's chiefs became popular in Canada near then end of the 1800's. They were introduced from the Dakota people of the United States.

A winter dress was put away until the first snowfall.

The Dream-Catcher

Dream-catchers are delicately woven webs said to act as powerful protectors and to hold bad dreams at bay. To use the gossamer hoop is a simple task. Mount the catcher in a bedroom window. During the blackest part of the night, bad dreams become tangled in the web. During the day, the unpleasant dream is burned off by the reassuring light of the sun. The fragile catcher is clean and ready for further use. Dream catchers originated in the Ojibway tradition and can be obtained at native craft stores.

NATIVE ARTS AND CRAFTS: EDMONTON

ABOVE: Traditional prairie arts stand picturesquely in a grouping high above conventional craft items (not shown). Since there are sacred objects hidden among these items, special permission was required to take this photograph.
INSET: Prairie artists continue to create new types of designs for ornamenting buckskin items.

Etchings, serigraphs, and originals by many modern native artists are on display in various Edmonton galleries. Original works by emerging artists such as John Littlechild, Rick Beaver, Maxine Noel, and Jim Logan are setting a new standard for native art. With its position as a gateway to the north, Edmonton is a good place to investigate Inuit soapstone carvings, limited edition prints from Cape Dorset, tapestries from Pangnirtung of the eastern Arctic, and other examples of northern art. Some galleries sell masks, wooden carvings, and jewellery from a wide variey of traditions. Southwestern Navaho turquoise may be displayed alongside west coast engraved sterling silver. Some of the northern craft forms of note are Déné and Slavey moccasins, moose-hair tuft barettes, and mukluks. Moose-hair tuft ornaments are made from dyed moose whiskers; mukluks are knee-high moccasins. Beadwork was either floral or geometric. Some shops also sell steatite sculptures. Steatite was originally used to make stone peacepipes, but is now used for other art forms. Eskimo (Inuit) duffle jackets and beaded belts are also notable as types of northern apparel.

Native Arts: Edmonton

Alberta Indian Arts and Crafts Society Show
Annually each August
(403) 426-2048

Bearclaw Gallery,
9724 – 111 Ave, Edmonton
(403) 479-8502

Fort Door Indian Crafts, 10308 81 Ave, Edmonton
(403) 432-7535

Front Gallery, 12302 Jasper Ave, Edmonton
(403) 488-2952

Indian Trader, West Edmonton Mall, Edmonton
(403) 444-1165

Native Endeavours, 10715 - 152 Street, Edmonton
(403) 486-0069

Northern Images, Parklane, West Edmonton Mall, Edmonton
(403) 444-1995

BUFFALO PRESERVE: ELK ISLAND NATIONAL PARK

In the past, hundreds of thousands of bison roamed the plains of the western Canada.

P arks such as Elk Island National Park and Wood Buffalo National Park were both founded in the 1920s with the good intention of preserving the last of the buffalo herds. But at the start, several blunders were made. When herds outgrew their southern pastures, they were transferred between parks. Some were Plains Bisons and some were Wood Bison, which are larger and darker. These two distinct subspecies were inadvertantly mixed; a few animals carried diseases. Subsequent interbreeding increased the spread of tuberculosis and brucellosis, thereby weakening the animals, which at the time were not recognized as different lines. Unfortunately, at present a number of individuals are still chronically ill. Nearby cattle farmers want the herd destroyed but Treaty 8 bands and many scientists disagree. The herds have developed a natural resistance; some offspring are not showing signs of disease. However more than 40,000 diseased bison have been destroyed in the last decade.

At Elk Island National Park, the buffalo are healthy and breed well. Elk Island National Park is located 45 km east of Edmonton on Highway 16. Motorists drive a circuit

Lac Ste. Anne Pilgrimage

In the 1800s, a group of devout native people travelled a great distance to be christened at the mission here. A re-creation of the pligrimage is held each year in July. Thousands of native and non-native people walk the Lac Ste. Anne Trail. Information is available from the Village of Onoway, (403) 967-5338.

around the park. The Astotin Interpretive Centre sponsors nature programs; phone ahead. Information is available from Elk Island National Park, (403) 992-6338, recording (403) 922-5790, fax (403) 998-3686.

Wood Buffalo National Park is also a UNESCO World Heritage Site. Larger than Switzerland, it is one of the largest national parks anywhere in the world. It straddles the boundry of Alberta and the Northwest Territories (NWT). The first people here were the Beaver and Slavey, but they were later supplanted by the Cree and Chipewyan, who moved west with the fur trade. Fort Chipewyan, established in 1788, is the oldest continuously inhabited settlement in Alberta. Information can be obtained from the park superintendent (403) 872-2349, Fort Smith, NWT, or from Parks Canada or Tourism Alberta.

Big Knife Provincial Park: Battle River

More than 200 years ago, this area was in dispute between the Blackfoot Confederacy and the Cree Nations. As long-time traditional enemies, there were many skirmishes between them. According to native stories, two famous warriors— Big Man, a Cree, and Knife, a Blackfoot—finally met each other at this place. Both fought to the death in a ferocious battle.

Many years ago, along this quiet stretch of river, old enmities were made right only to be replaced with new bitterness. The imbalances between native tribes never resolved themselves, but were finally interrupted by white man's presence.

Today, the creek is known as "Big Knife" in honour of both warriors.

War was a frequent occurrence between plains groups, but it was not practised in the sense usually understood by outsiders. Bravery rather than agression was recognized, and killing was rarely accorded honour. The taking of an enemy's weapon earned the highest honour, the taking of a scalp second, and the capture of a horse third. Scalping did not necessarily result in death for the victim.

In many skirmishes, the acts were symbolic. It was considered an act of bravery to ride across open country and, finding an enemy, to merely touch him. This was known as "counting coup." For warfare to escalate into a full-scale massacre where lives were lost, was a rare occurrence.

For this reason, Big Knife is honoured as an exception, rather than the rule.

Big Knife Provincial Park is a small picnic area located on Highway 855 between Halkirk and Heisler. Information is available from the Battle River Tourist Association, Box 1515, Camrose, AB T4V 1X4, (403) 672-8555, fax (403) 672-0711.

The tomahawk, a well-balanced weapon, is often portrayed incorrectly in Hollywood movies.

Small Native Artifact Collections: Central and Northern Alberta

Wetaskiwin and District Museum	Wetaskiwin
Museé Heritage Museum	St. Albert
Sodbuster's Archives and Museum	Strome
Fort Chipewyan Bicentennial Museum	Fort Chipewyan
Girouxville Museum	Girouxville
Native Cultural Arts Museum	Grouard
Centennial Museum and Archives	Peace River
Cultural Museum	Saddle Lake
High Prairie and District Museum	High Prairie
Slave Lake Native Friendship Centre	Slave Lake

Information is available from Alberta Tourism, 1-800-661-8888, (403) 427-4321.

ST. MARY'S CHURCH: RED DEER

In 1966, Father Werner Manx, an Oblate priest born in Germany, placed his faith in a Blackfoot architect (considered an outsider) to design his new church. That architect has gone on to an outstanding career crowned by his acclaimed design for the Canadian Museum of Civilization in Ottawa.

Douglas Cardinal's career might be characterized as the fire of vision combined with an eagerness to avoid rectangles. The geography of the Battle River valley is said to be infused into all of his work.

Visitors can best appreciate St. Mary's by circling it before entering. Various roof slopes appear and disappear. It becomes obvious why the computer calculations for the roof design were contracted out to a major American university. The three voids in the campanile are to be occupied with three bells when the parish can afford them. The spiral design is based on the seven sacraments, with baptism visible from the outside. "The altar," says Cardinal, "is dressed not in silk, but in rough linen."

At one point in his career, Cardinal studied the native cultures of New Mexico and was greatly influenced in Texas. After a physically exhausting period in the

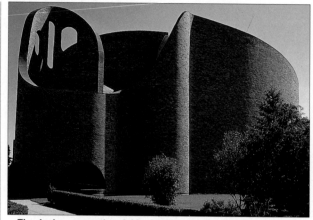

The design soars, then folds; it spirals as if on outstretched wing and speaks of forces greater than the human reach. St. Mary's Church in Red Deer is an architectural masterpiece.

I don't design boxes.
—Douglas Cardinal, Blackfoot, 1987

1970s, he accompanied Chief Robert Smallboy to a native camp in the shadow of the Rocky Mountains. There he undertook sweats, fasts, and healing. Cardinal also studied for a period under an Arapahoe medicine man. These aboriginal experiences made an impact on Cardinal's architectural interpretations. The

sacred circle, so important in native cultures, is reflected in all his designs.

Information on St. Mary's is available from the David Thompson Tourist Council, 4836 Ross Street, Red Deer, AB T4N 5E8, (403) 342-2032.

Camera Safari: Cardinal's Architecture

Cardinal's Own Studio ....Stoney Plain
St. Mary's Church ....Red Deer
Stettler Hospital...Stettler
Grand Prairie Regional College and Theatre..........................Grand Prairie
Ponoka Provincial Building..Ponoka
Kehewin Indian Village ....Grouard
Indian Métis Rehabilitation Centre...Bonnyville
St. Albert Place..St. Albert
Canadian Museum of Civilization...Ottawa, Ontario

RIBSTONES HISTORIC SITE: VIKING

Two white quartzite stones, important in Cree hunting rituals, are found among similiar stones placed on this sacred site. Centimetre-deep designs depict the buffalo's backbone and ribs. They were abraded at least 1000 years ago. The rocks represent two buffalo—one female, one male.

From atop the glacial knoll, one can view the flat prairie spreading out in all directions. Hunting parties standing atop this small hill could survey about 250 sq km of territory. If the migrating herds were anywhere in the vicinity, they were tracked.

After a kill, certain bison were brought back to the site. Here, sacrifices were made and rituals performed to ensure further successful hunts and the continued fertility of the buffalo. The sacred paraphernalia associated with this ceremony included such items as a medicine pipe, sweetgrass or pine needles, a rattle, buffalo fur, red clay powder, and the stones them-

These stationary white stones are silent testimonies to the disappearance of the buffalo—but the *spirits* of the great behemoths continue to graze on the prairies.

selves.

When settlers arrived in the area about 1900, the stones were still in use. Natives regularly left offerings of beads, tobacco, and meat for the stones. To the present day, it is not unusual to come across flowers, mushrooms, and other tiny remembrances left as offerings.

The stones are located on a side road near Kinsella. To find them, travel 8 km south of Viking to Junction 26/36, then to side road 615. Travel 11.7 km, then turn south. Travel 2.4 km. There are small arrow markers indicating the site. Information is available from the Battle River Tourist Association, Box 1515, Camrose, AB T4V 1X4, (403) 672-8555.

Special Tours: Departures from Northern Alberta

Athabaska Delta Interpretive Tours, Box 178, Fort Chipewyan, AB T0P 1B0, (403) 679-3929, fax (403) 679-3826; by boat, 8 hours on historic waterways; or wilderness vacation overnight packages.

Blair Jean Wilderness Tours, 13 MacIver St, Fort MacMurray, AB T9H 2Z6, (403) 791-4500; by jetboat and land, weekend seclusion packages, stay in log cabins.

Chincaga River Tours, Box 40, Manning, AB T0H 2M0, no phone available; by river boat, 1 to 7 days, wildlife and bird viewing.

Sub Arctic Wilderness Adventures, Box 685, Fort Smith, NWT X0E 0P0, (403) 872-2467; by dog sled, 7 to 13 days, stay with local families; also trekking in Wood Buffalo National Park; adventure gear rentals.

Tar Island River Cruises, Box 5070, Peace River, AB T8S 1R7, (403) 624-4295; by jet boat; 1 day along the Peace River with barbeque; hunt for fossils.

Recommended Reading

Bancroft-Hunt, Norman, *North American Indians,* Philadelphia, Courage Books, 1992

Barry, P.S., *Mystical Themes in Milk River Rock Art,* Edmonton, University of Alberta Press, 1991

Colombo, John Robert, *Songs of the Indians,* Part I and Part II, Ottawa, Multiculturalism Directorate of the Government of Canada, 1983

Clark, Ella Elizabeth, *Indian Legends of Canada,* Toronto, McClelland and Stewart Ltd, 1974

Daley, Richard and Chris Arnett, *They Write Their Dreams on the Rock Forever,* Vancouver, Talonbooks, 1993

Fagan, Brian M., *People of the Earth,* Glenview Illinois, Scott, Foremand and Company, 1989

Foster, John and Dick Harrison and I.S. MacLaren, *Buffalo,* Edmonton, University of Alberta Press, 1992

Harris, Robert Charles, *The Best of B.C.'s Hiking Trails,* Vancouver, MacLean Hunter, 1986

Indian and Northern Affairs Canada, *The Canadian Indian,* Minister of Supply and Services Canada, 1990

Jensen, Vicki, *Where The People Gather,* Vancouver/ Toronto, Douglas and McIntyre, 1992

Kew, Della and P.E. Goddard, *Indian Art and Culture of the Northwest Coast,* North Vancouver B.C., Hancock House Publishers, 1974

Kramer, Pat, *B.C. For Free and Almost Free,* Vancouver, Whitecap Books, 1993

Kramer, Pat, *Understanding Totems,* Banff, Altitude Publishing, 1995

MacDonald, Joanne, *Gitwangak Village Life, A Museum Collection,* Hull Quebec, Canadian Government Publishing Centre, 1984

Macaree, Mary and David, *109 Walks in B.C.'s Lower Mainland,* Seattle, The Mountaineers, 1976

MacMillan, Alan D., *Native Peoples and Cultures of Canada: An Anthropological Overview,* Vancouver/ Toronto, Douglas and McIntyre, 1988

Paquet, Maggie M. 1990, *Parks of British Columbia and The Yukon.* MAIA Publishing Ltd. N. Vancouver

Patton, Brian and Bart Robinson, *The Canadian Rockies Trail Guide,* Banff, Summerthought Ltd., 1986

Rothenburger, Mel, *The Chilcotin War,* Langley B.C., Mr. Paperback, 1978

Stewart, Hilary, *Indian Fishing,* Vancouver/Toronto, Douglas and McIntyre, 1982

Stewart, Hilary, *Looking at Totem Poles,* Vancouver/ Toronto, Douglas and McIntyre, 1993

Stewart, Hilary, *The Adventures and Sufferings of John R. Jewitt Captive of Maquinna,* Vancouver/ Toronto, Douglas and McIntyre, 1987

Turner, Nancy Dr., *Plants in B.C. Indian Technology,* B.C. Provincial Museum Handbooks, Victoria, Queens Printer, 1991

Turner, Nancy Dr., *Food Plants of Coastal Peoples,* Part 1 and Part 2, B.C. Provincial Museum Handbooks, Victoria, Queens Printer, 1991

Vancouver Art Gallery, *Emily Carr,* North Vancouver, J.J. Douglas Ltd., 1977

Whyte, Jon, *Indians of the Rockies,* Banff, Altitude Publishing, 1985

INDEX

INDEX

Index

THE AUTHOR

"I came to feel the book was more than just a project," says Pat Kramer, "it became an initiate's journey." Surviving a tornado right after taking photos of the medicine wheel stones was only slightly less nerve-racking than encountering bears while photographing the sweat lodge. Though she arrived unannounced in Kitwancool, one of the elders approached her and related a long story. "A wind that blows too much, blows off course," he said. Pat took it to mean she should not reveal everything she discovered during her journeys. But much she does reveal, with the permission of her native contacts, more than enough to get readers started on their own journeys.

Pat Kramer first worked with native people during a graduate research project in Alberta. Long since a transplant to the BC coast, she now instructs at the Native Education Centre. There she values the friendship of her native students who seek to start their own tourism operations. "I hope this book, in some small way, supports native tourism ventures," she says.

When she is not busy teaching and writing, she leads special interest tours. Ranging from ancient cliff cities in Arizona, to searching for therapeutic hot-spring muds in northern BC, Pat has organized several exciting adventures. Now serving as President of the Western Tour Directors Association of Canada, she is also chair of an industry team that is setting standards for Canadian long-distance tour directors.

Pat's other books are *B.C. for Free, and Almost Free* published by Whitecap Books, and *Understanding Totems*, published by Altitude Publishing.